dult Side

Eco Effect™

The Greening of Money

Neale S. Godfrey
with Beth Polazzo

Visit our Web Site

www.eco-effect.net

Special thanks to the following people for ECHOing to me:

Dr. Rita Littrell, Michele Halsell, Kimberly Randle, Theres W. Steifer; Cécile Rothschild and Team; Rhett Godfrey; Hayley Bubb; Dennis Robertson; Carol Poteat-Buchanan; Steve Rust; Eric Martins; Joan Larkin; Angelo Rivello; Joe Russo; Jack Cox; Jesse Broome; Stan Smith; General Michael Rochelle; Mary Donohue; Carol Gattis; Kristin Ginty; Bob Safranek; Shea Mathis; and Michael Belkewitch.

ECO-Effect, Inc. is ECHOing by making donations to the U.S. National Committee for UNIFEM and Heifer International.

Eco Effect
The Greening of Money

Designed and illustrated by Create & Associates, Inc., a team of creative designers. Cécile Rothschild is an accomplished, award-winning designer with a rich history of helping clients solve business communication problems across many industries. Prior to founding her own firm, she worked at U.S. News and World Report as an art director and at Newsweek as a creative director. She hopes her 14 year old daughter, Léa, and her 12 year old son, Max, continue doing their part to incorporate sustainability into their everyday lives.

Her team of talented designers includes Berta Martinez, born in Cuba and raised in Spain. Berta's knowledge spans a broad range of industries, from insurance/financial services to consumer packaged goods and even to the children's market. She has also earned a Master's Degree in Communications Design from Pratt Institute. Included in the design and production was Mutsumi Hyuga and the wonderful illustrations from Jim Ryan.

Retail Price: $16.99

ECO-Effect: The Greening of Money.
2011 6th Printing

For information, please address:

Godfrey House, Inc.
31 Twinbrooks Trail
Chester, NJ 07930
Phone: 908-879-8898
neale@childrensfinancialnetwork.com

Library of Congress Cataloging – In – Publication Data: Godfrey, Neale S. with Polazzo, Beth
ECO-Effect: The Greening of Money – 2nd ed. Library of Congress Control Number: 2009903545

GODFREY HOUSE, INC.

We've ECHOed to you on 100% recycled paper that was printed in the U.S.A.

www.eco-effect.net

ISBN - 13: 978-0-61535-723-2
ISBN - 10: 0-61535-723-7

Some of Neale's Other Books...

FOR ADULTS

Money Doesn't Grow on Trees: A Parent's Guide to Raising Financially Responsible Children

Money Still Doesn't Grow on Trees: A Parent's Guide to Raising Financially Responsible Teenagers and Young Adults

A Penny Saved: Teaching Your Children the Values and Life Skills They Will Need to Live in the Real World

Making Change: A Woman's Guide to Designing Her Financial Future

Mom, Inc.: Taking Your Work Skills Home

FOR CHILDREN

Neale S. Godfrey's Ultimate Kids' Money Book

LIFE, Inc.: The Ultimate Career Guide for Young People

Why Money Was Invented

Here's the Scoop: Follow an Ice Cream Cone Around the World

A Money Adventure: Earning, Saving, Spending, Sharing

From Beads to Bank Notes: The Story of Money

Check It Out: The Book About Banking

Taking Stock: The World of Business

Neale S. Godfrey is an acknowledged expert on family and children's finances who has been in the financial field for more than 30 years. Early in her career, Neale became one of the first female executives at The Chase Manhattan Bank. Later, she became the president of The First Women's Bank and founder of The First Children's Bank.

In 1989, Neale formed her own company, Children's Financial Network, Inc., whose mission is to educate children and their parents about money. Neale is the author of 17 books that deal with money, life skills and value issues. Her groundbreaking book *Money Doesn't Grow on Trees: A Parent's Guide to Raising Financially Responsible Children* hit #1 on The New York Times Best Sellers list. Neale was also a syndicated columnist for the Associated Press and has published countless articles in newspapers and magazines throughout the country.

Her latest educational program, *LIFE, Inc.: The Ultimate Career Guide for Young People,* consists of the Career Guide Book, Teacher's Guide, Student Journal and Web site. This program, sponsored by the Deloitte Foundation, is reaching hundreds of thousands of students through organizations such as The United States Army, The National Guard, The National Urban League, YWCA, The Bureau of Indian Education, FCCLA, DECA, ASPIRA, etc.

Neale has often appeared as a financial expert on programs such as *The Oprah Winfrey Show, Good Morning America, Today*, CNBC, CNN. She is also Nickelodeon's financial expert on NickJr.com.

Neale has been honored with awards such as Woman of the Year, Banker of the Year, Child Advocate of the Year, Best 50 Women in Business in New Jersey and the Femme Award. Neale was also named National Winner of the Ascendancy Award for Business Women.

Neale lives in Chester, New Jersey, and is the proud mother of two children...and an even prouder grandma!

Beth Polazzo is an experienced, award-winning writer who has worked for television (WPIX-TV and WCBS-TV), newspapers (The New York Times and Dow Jones) and Newsweek magazine.

Recently, Beth formed The Polazzo Group, doing freelance work for diverse clients on a multitude of topics. One of her greatest strengths is her creativity and ability to make the complicated seem simple to understand.

When it comes to ECOlogy, Beth's father passed along his love of forestry and conservation way before it was "in." This has translated into her passion for the ECO-EFFECT.

Among her other talents, Beth is an avid dressage rider, which makes her an expert on "horse power."

She lives in a brownstone in Brooklyn with Howard and 3 feral cats. Beth adores being a mom and a two-time nana.

Eco Effect™
The Greening of Money

To our children and their spouses—
Kyle and Art Godfrey-Ryan, Rhett Godfrey,
Matt Polazzo and Linda Fan—with love.
We are so proud of you and hope that you
will continue making a difference in the world
by ECHOing your ECOlogical and
ECOnomic ideas to the next generation.

Panasonic
ideas for life

eco ideas

A MESSAGE FROM JOSEPH M. TAYLOR
Chairman and Chief Executive Officer, Panasonic Corporation of North America

Dear Reader,

On behalf of Panasonic, I would like to thank you for doing your part to help make our world more environmentally sustainable. By reading this book and taking part in the many activities provided, you are joining a large group of people, schools, households, and companies (such as Panasonic) that are taking steps toward improving our planet's health.

Looking toward 2018, Panasonic's 100th anniversary, our company seeks to become the # 1 Green Innovation Company in the electronics industry. Our goal is nothing less than to create a comfortable and practical, but Zero Carbon Emission, lifestyle through our products and technologies.

Panasonic understands that the Earth's resources are limited and is committed to the sustainable use of those resources as well as the protection of biodiversity and a healthy ecology around the planet. We want not only to reduce emissions in our own offices and factories across the globe, but to help you to be able to do the same. Panasonic is dedicated to bringing clean and green technology into homes, schools, offices, and transportation systems around the world through energy and cost efficient devices, energy generation systems and recyclable products, and eco-innovations.

Panasonic's goal is also to grant future generations the gift of empowerment through education. It is imperative that our future leaders understand the importance of an environmentally sustainable society. By partnering with ECO-Effect®, Panasonic seeks to encourage students, families, and other companies to minimize their carbon footprints, to become stewards of the earth and to send their own ECHOs around the world.

About Panasonic Corporation of North America

Based in Secaucus, NJ, Panasonic Corporation of North America provides a broad line of digital and other electronics products for consumer, business and industrial use. The company is the principal North American subsidiary of Osaka, Japan-based Panasonic Corporation (NYSE: PC), and the hub of Panasonic's U.S. branding, marketing, sales, service and R&D operations. Panasonic ranked number 10 on Interbrand's Top 50 Best Global Brands 2011 survey. Globally the company is pledged to practice prudent, sustainable use of the earth's natural resources and protect our environment through the company's Eco Ideas programs. As part of its continuing efforts to reduce its carbon footprint, Panasonic Corporation of North America will relocate its operations to a new eco-efficient office tower adjacent to a mass transit hub in Newark, NJ in 2013. Information about Panasonic Eco Ideas initiatives is available at http://panasonic.net/eco/ecoideas. Information about Panasonic and its products is available at www.panasonic.com.
Additional company information for journalists is also available at www.panasonic.com/pressroom.

Panasonic
ideas for life

eco ideas

A MESSAGE FROM DAVID THOMPSON
Director Corporate Environmental Department, Panasonic Corporation of North America

Dear Reader,

As the Director of Panasonic's Environmental Department, I would like to thank you for taking the first step toward a greener lifestyle. We at Panasonic are working hard to promote environmental innovations and ideas. For example, did you know that Panasonic is developing a house with virtually zero carbon emissions! By using materials that insulate well, energy efficient appliances, and a combination of fuel cells, a solar power generator, and accumulator batteries to create and store energy, the house of the future is already well on it's way to becoming a reality.

But, we're not just looking to help home owners reduce carbon emissions; we intend to do the same at our sites around the world. We have already significantly reduced our emissions and have developed a plan to continue doing so for a much cleaner future. By 2019 Panasonic is aiming to reduce our CO2 emissions by approximately 120 million tons and we are well on our way to generating zero waste emissions from our plants by that same year.

These changes are large scale, but we're looking to you to help on a small scale. ECO-Effect® offers many ways to make small changes in your lifestyle that will have a significant effect on our environment. We at Panasonic encourage you to try out some of the techniques offered in this book to reduce your carbon footprint and promote environmental stewardship.

The steps to a greener lifestyle are easy and most can be done within the comfort of your home. By getting your school, home, and community involved in the ECO-Effect® program you can help spread the word about taking care of our world.

On behalf of the Panasonic Environmental Department and everyone at Panasonic, I would like to congratulate you on your eco-leadership! Enjoy the book!

TABLE OF CONTENTS

About Neale

OK, So Who Am I?

You may have seen my New York Times #1 Best Seller *Money Doesn't Grow on Trees: A Parent's Guide To Raising Financially Responsible Children* or a host of other financially related books that I've written for kids and their families. Two of my books also teach women how to make financial lifestyle changes that will help them deal with rotten situations like divorce, death and raising teenage children (and not necessarily in that order).

My newest book, which is sponsored by the Deloitte Foundation, is called *LIFE, Inc.: The Ultimate Career Guide for Young People* and includes a matching curriculum. The *LIFE*, Inc. program serves hundreds of thousands of students, and the Web Site at www.nealeslifeinc.com will reach millions more.

Perhaps you've seen me on *The Oprah Winfrey Show, Today, Good Morning America*, CNN or CNBC.

You might also recognize my name from newspaper articles about kids and money that I wrote when I was a syndicated columnist for the Associated Press. I was also the president of The First Women's Bank and founder of The First Children's Bank at FAO Schwarz. Currently, as the Chairman of Children's Financial Network, Inc., a company I founded 20 years ago, my mission is to empower children and their parents to take charge of their financial lives.

As I continue on this journey, my interests and activities continue to multiply, from working toward women's empowerment and gender equality as an active board member of the U.S. National Committee for UNIFEM, to working with the National Urban League, ASPIRA, the YWCA and the U.S. Army. I've basically "been there, done that." However, one common thread runs throughout all my experiences: The lessons of financial exchange can be applied to social change.

Until recently, I, (sometimes referred to as "The Goddess of Money") never realized just how enormous the connection is between ECOnomics and ECOlogy. Both money and the environment are green... at least here in the United States.

What Do I Believe About Money?

Money doesn't exist in a vacuum. The creation, use or misuse of every service or good impacts everyone...and everyone has an impact on our environment. The ECOnomic circulation of money can be likened to the ECOlogical circulation of resources. Both involve social choices. Both also involve lessons (either by example or education) that start in the home.

F.Y.I.:

In fact, the word "echo" comes from the ancient Greek word "oikos," which means house.

Teaching children about money is not about turning them into Ebenezer Scrooges. Money is about values, about relationships, about choices, about self-esteem. You know, as well as I do, that the same dollar that's used to buy drugs can be given to charity...and that decision affects society. The money for a candy bar... either given or withheld...could have been put aside for a computer or even put into a college savings fund... but by just giving the money without careful thought or explanation, a child may not only become spoiled, but they may also be misinformed when it comes to making financial decisions.

When I started working on the topic of kids and money in the 1980s, lots of people said, "We are dealing with the 'I want, I want' generation...how can we even *start* teaching our kids about the value, purpose and meaning of money?" I made it simple—start by teaching kids the natural consequences of money. The only way to get it is to earn it—there is no entitlement program in life.

As I said a few paragraphs ago, money is always a social issue—it never exists in isolation. You can: *EARN it, SAVE it, SPEND it, SHARE it.*

Whatever you do with it, money has consequences that are both personal and global.

Unless you have an illegal printing press or you inherit a fortune, you can't get or *EARN* money by yourself. You have to make a social contract with someone else and then fulfill your end of that deal. For example, to earn money, it might mean going out and getting a job at which you agree to do certain tasks in exchange for a salary (money and benefits). In essence, there are always buyers and sellers, manufacturers or growers, each making financial decisions that affect a chain of social dynamics.

You can *SAVE* it alone, but that's an intermediate step before you actually use the money. By the way, a sound financial plan—even in this economy—does not include putting your dollars under the mattress. A better idea is to use professional investing assistance, which means you now have another social contract. You may then have to deal with people who are bankers and investors.

You can't *SPEND* it alone; you have to go back into society and decide where and how you'll use it. Some of it is not your choice, like paying taxes. However, if you think of money as a finite resource, which most of us do, you have a better chance of staying within your budget.

To *SHARE* money means to understand how much you can afford to give and then donate to a socially valuable cause. You can choose to save the penguins, donate to Heifer International, give to the U.S. National Committee for UNIFEM, tithe to your church, or give tzedakah to your synagogue. Whatever your cause is, charitable giving provides a feeling of self-worth and a sense of connection to your community and the world.

You can get money in bad ways—like stealing it. You can spend money in bad or irresponsible ways—like buying more than you can afford. You can save money in bad ways—like hoarding it. You can even give it away in bad ways—like trying to buy popularity.

For better or worse, money is one of the connective tissues that hold society together.

Putting Money to Work

After you earn money, you have to budget it for savings/investing, spending and sharing. I taught children, as young as three, to do simple chores to earn an allowance. But there are two types of chores: Citizen-of-the-Household and Work-For-Pay.

Work-For-Pay Chores are just that—money is the consequence of work. Conversely, Citizen-of-the-Household Chores are done without monetary compensation. You teach your children that, as "good" household members, they contribute and share. Even at that young age they can learn, for example, to pick up their things because that's what respectful members of the household do.

If we take this behavior one step further and think of good Citizen-of-the-Community Chores, it would mean that you would pick up and properly dispose of litter you see on the sidewalk or in the woods. Moreover, you wouldn't expect to be paid for your actions.

In the ECO-EFFECT, we'll help you to teach your kids—and your kids to teach you—to "ECHO" to the community, schools, businesses and government... and to be good Citizens-of-the-World.

In Greek mythology, Echo was a nymph who was spurned by Narcissus and pined away until only her voice remained. But, unlike Narcissus, not only will your voice remain, your deeds will as well. So, when we use the word "ECHO," what we are referring to is the repetition and sharing of sound ECOnomic and ECOlogical ideas to family members, friends, classmates, business associates, the community and even to the world. We hope that you will pass along (or ECHO) your ideas and welcome new ones, thus creating a wave of concern and knowledge that will continue to grow and help the world become a far better place for us to live.

It's an easy step from ECOnomics to ECOlogy; neither exists in isolation and both are interrelated. Your ECOnomic decisions *are* world decisions and your ECOlogical decisions *are* world decisions. So, let's see if we can now apply what we've learned about money and create a loud and clear ECO-EFFECT. Join us and create your own ECHO.

What Does Global Warming Have to Do With the Crazy Weather Outside?

Scientists agree that the average temperature of the earth is rising (almost 1 degree Celsius in the past 100 years!). The 11 hottest years on record have occurred in the past 12 years. This extreme change in temperature has led to some big changes in the weather we experience everyday.

Global Warming, or Climate Change as some prefer to call it, is not just more beach days. This shift in weather patterns has led to a huge increase in precipitation (including snow) in some places, and floods, droughts and tropical storms in others.

We can all do our part to help mitigate the effects of Climate Change by reducing our own emissions through the use of energy efficient appliances, eco-conscious transportation, and creating less waste.

F.Y.I.:

Walking the Walk

Over the years, I have worked to reduce my carbon footprint. Now, with the help of REC Solar and Tom Pickert, I am excited to join the Green Revolution by putting up a 9 kW Solar System on my house. It will not only help me reduce my cost of purchasing electricity from the electric utility, but by going solar I will be using clean, GREEN, and renewable energy from the sun. To get more information on how solar can work for you, reach out to my friends at REC Solar by going to www.recsolar.com/ECO.

Chapter One

The ECO-EFFECT—Why You?

If you're like most of us, you can get so bogged down just thinking about all that needs to be done to "save the planet" that you may do nothing at all. Even in your own home, considering all the ways that you might save energy can be overwhelming. It's easy to hear all this "noise" and just want to "tune out" instead.

I want you to "stay tuned," so I'm going to set one simple ground rule: We *will* celebrate steps being taken to improve the home, school, community, workplace, country and the world. We will *not* criticize, expose or condemn anyone.

Do we have all the answers—of course not. However, with the ECO-EFFECT, we hope to raise consciousness, be inclusive and have you take steps together with your family. We will link generations, corporations, towns and schools, nationally and internationally. We will attempt to start a working dialogue...an ECHOing of ideas, questions and possible solutions but most importantly, we want you to take action.

The good news is that we aren't starting from scratch. Scientists and many other people have made us aware of our ECOlogical fragility. "Green" is part of our lexicon. A day doesn't go by without a news report about water pollution, greenhouse gases, pesticides, global warming, mercury in our fish, dying reefs, holes in the ozone layer, lead and asbestos poisonings, toxic chemicals in our clothing and cleaning products, and on and on and on.

If this news makes you feel uneasy, it should. We did it to ourselves. We may not have known that what we were doing was "bad," but now there's no excuse for playing ostrich. We did these things. We own them. Now we need to change our behaviors and clean up our acts—literally! We'll help you do it. Each of us can make a difference—one step, one person, one home at a time.

Easter Island – "ECO-Eden Gone Awry"

Several thousand years ago, the indigenous people of this Polynesian Island, lived amid forests filled with all they needed to live. They are noted for their enormous statues called "moais," that were carved from local quarries. In order to move them to where they were supposed to be, the men had to cut down the trees and create sleds and ladders. What they never thought about was what would happen after the last tree was cut down. What happened? Their ECO-Eden was destroyed.

"Darned-If-You-Do, Darned-If-You-Don't"

Just in case you've been hiding under a rock for the last few decades, here are a few examples of what humans have done to the environment and how they've reacted:

In the United States, we're a nation of "stuff." We want stuff, we produce stuff and then we throw stuff away and call it "garbage." We used to burn a lot of garbage until it was pointed out that we were polluting the air. So we doused the fires and started creating "landfills" of garbage. However, they attracted flies and rodents, smelled awful, and, guess what...they *still* caused pollution. We tried moving the landfills to locations where many people wouldn't see or smell them, but the pollution kept leaking into the air, the ground and even the water supply. So, what was our next idea? We put our garbage on barges and sent it to places where we thought people might not notice or care.

Well, they *did*—and we *do*.

Every day, the earth's population grows; creating a demand for even more stuff that will eventually end up as garbage. What's a consumer to do? It's a "Darned-If-You-Do, Darned-If-You-Don't" dilemma. Even worse, it may cause a reaction of, "I'll be wrong no matter what I do, so I'll do nothing."

This attitude is not good. A case in point is the issue of how to carry stuff home from the grocery store. Most of us used to think that paper bags were the most environmentally correct choice because of paper's solid reputation as a great renewable product. Plastic bags, on the other hand, garnered a somewhat negative reputation because they are generally made from non-renewable resources, such as petroleum or natural gas. As it turns out, though, both have their advantages and disadvantages. In fact, plastic bags can be recycled. What do you do? Well, you can just take what they give you at the checkout counter with the "darned-if-you-do, darned-if-you don't" attitude, or you might opt for a third choice–reusable, washable shopping bags. Of course, ECOnomically they cost more, but they do have less of an ECOlogical impact.

How about hybrid or electric cars? Hybrids sound like they'd be environmentally friendly since they use less gas and cause less pollution. However, they cost more to buy, and some studies show that the batteries in these cars are environmentally harmful. What do we do, then? Perhaps, we do nothing. It's not that we don't *want* to do something; we just don't know the *right* thing to do.

Well, for starters, you could check the web site www.fueleconomy.gov to calculate how many years it would take for a hybrid to pay for itself or you can just wait around until the "perfect" car is invented.

One thing is for sure though: Any state of uncertainty is stressful. We all have *more than* enough stress in our lives: children, job security, health care costs, elderly care, divorce, finances, retirement...(I'm depressing myself–need I continue?)

Why should you worry about anything more than your *own* problems? Because you must–like it or not, it is *our* world. There was a saying from the 1960s that went, "If you're not part of the solution, you're part of the problem." This saying still rings true today.

Taking Ownership

Global problems are *all* of our problems. It may not seem that the "paper or plastic" issue is all that pressing when you are still at the office at 10 p.m. and your phone rings. You think it's your kids calling to ask how to warm the meatloaf in the microwave–but no, it's the police. The officer lets you know that your children are at the station because they decided to share the cold meatloaf with 20 other underage friends—all of whom thought the main course might taste better with beer! *Now* would be a good time to leave your office. I'm with you—the "paper or plastic" issue is not your biggest problem at this particular moment.

However, maybe in a week or a month—when you stop having fantasies about launching your teens into outer space on the next space shuttle to Mars (is it booked?) and have stopped wondering, "What was I thinking when I thought having children and a full-time job would be a breeze?"—maybe, just maybe, the ECO-EFFECT will be back in your consciousness.

Why? Well, isn't there a part of you that wants to ECHO to the world (I'm not talking about all your frustrations and anger, I'm talking about the good things) and ECHO to your kids (when you're speaking to them again)? You do have values that you want them to appreciate, and even if it's not on a daily basis, you do care about the world. You know it is part of your legacy.

Since we all have contributed to the Earth's problems, it's up to all of us to accept responsibility and then do something to change our ways. In short, we have to take ownership for what we've done and we hope that you can ECHO to your kids that they need to "step up to the plate," as well.

On a micro, day-to-day level, you want them to take responsibility for the meatloaf-and-beer fest. You really don't want to hear, "It wasn't my fault—my friends brought over the beer. I had to drink it or else I'd look like a loser...blah, blah, blah."

On a macro level, the conversation is essentially the same. Whatever the state of the world—we did it, we own it, and we all need to change our behavior.

Don't Walk Away

Of course, you can always do *nothing*—it's your choice. You can let someone else worry about it. As an alternative, let's put it in perspective. Maybe you don't worry about teens driving under the influence of illegal substances. Hey, it's not *your* problem—you don't even have teens, right? Be that as it may, it will most certainly become your problem if that drunk-driving teen hits you or someone you love.

Yet another option is to look the other way and simply adapt to the changing situations, like the ancient Trojans did. It is said that they let the trash build up on the floors of their homes and, every once in a while, covered it with dirt. As the floors got higher off the ground, and they had trouble standing straight, they just raised the roof and rebuilt the doors.

You can even try to walk away from it all, like Henry David Thoreau did in the mid-1800s. In effect, he dropped out, sat at Walden Pond and wrote great things. It was easier for him to "drop out," though, because he didn't have to give up cell phones, microwaves, PCs, fax machines, etc. In fact, he didn't have to give up *anything* with a plug or charger. I'm not "knocking" Henry—he was on to the concept of "less is more." We are a nation of *stuff*, and we are willing to pay for innovations that save time and effort. These same innovations supposedly increase our standard of living, yet—if you're anything like me—I feel like I spend even more time and effort dealing with them!

However, even if you're giving thought to dropping out like Thoreau, the acid rain is still falling, the ozone hole is still there, and the icebergs are still melting. In a parallel manner, you may take your vacation and "get away from it all," however, *your* mortgage is still ticking, *your* credit cards are still running up interest, and *your* car payments are mounting. These things are happening even if you don't think about them. So, we don't really have the option to drop out. You have to stay engaged, be a responsible parent and ECHO to your kids, your community, and the world.

Chapter Two

Getting Started—ECO-IQ

ECO-EFFECT Disclaimer

Many of the facts in this book have been ECHOed to us from various sources, which are referenced in the back of the book. You (parents, kids, schools, corporations and friends) are individually responsible for your own actions to determine what works for you and what doesn't. Why the disclaimer? If you decide to use candles to light your home instead of using electricity by turning on the lights, don't contact me (or my attorney, Eric) when the cat singes its tail!

Drop *In*. Don't Drop *Out*—Green Parenting

Do what you can and don't give up simply because the big picture seems overwhelming. Don't fight about plastic or paper but *do* help to bring awareness of the issues to your kids. Encourage them to bring ideas to you. Remember, action begins with raising consciousness about the issues—starting the ECHO.

Think about all the conflicting health stories we hear and read. Things that are declared *good* for us one day are declared *bad* for us the next. At least these conflicting stories help us become aware of what we put in our mouths. Remember: "You are what you eat." (That makes *me* a hot fudge sundae!)

Well, in the same way that we are responsible for what we eat, we are responsible for what we do while we're here on this planet. We don't own Earth, we are just passing through. The manner in which we leave the world to the next generation is part of our legacy, and it begins with how we treat one another and share our resources.

If you were to make a list of just *some* of the things that we've done to the planet, there's little doubt that you'd be so overwhelmed that you'd sit back, sigh and do nothing. The problem seems insurmountable—so, we're not going to waste time and effort talking about what's *not* being done. We're going to celebrate what you *are* doing and share what we *can do* together by ECHOing among ourselves, our communities and our world.

We can no longer claim "not knowing" as a reason for inaction. From the printed page to television and computer screens, there is no longer an excuse for ignorance as to what is going on in the world, as well as in your own community and your own home.

The only requirement is that you don't drop out on us. We are all connected, and we can't afford any weak or broken links. In the same way that we are all ECOomically connected, we are also ECOlogically connected. Money must be truly "green." My ozone hole is *yours* and *your* pollution is mine. All problems are *ours*, as we are *all* connected. It's time to take action and ECHO.

ECO-IQ: How Strong Is Your ECHO? Take this simple quiz and find out!

1. What is *Recycling?*
a. A ferris wheel going in reverse.
b. Biking back to the store to pick up the packages that you left there accidentally.
c. Reusing stuff.

2. What are *Greenhouse Gases?*
a. The results of the "Jolly Green Giant" eating too many beans at the barbeque.
b. The smells from the gym's locker room.
c. Carbon dioxide (CO_2), methane (yes, burps and farts), water vapor and other gases that let sunlight in and prevent heat from escaping.

3. What is the *Ozone Hole?*
a. What Dorothy fell into after leaving Kansas.
b. What your son's socks look like today.
c. It is not technically a "hole," but is a very thin layer of ozone in the stratosphere over the Antarctic where more protective ozone should exist.

4. What is a *Landfill?*
a. Extensive dental work.
b. When you've "had it" with your in-ground swimming pool.
c. A nice name for a dump or trash site.

5. What is a *Carbon Footprint?*
a. What Sasquatch leaves behind.
b. The mark left when you tried to fix your old typewriter with your feet.
c. The amount of carbon dioxide (CO_2) that comes from the energy we use.

6. What is *Alternative Energy?*
a. Jogging in a green Speedo.
b. Aging hippies kicking their feet in a hot tub.
c. Energy that is not created from fossil fuels, such as wind or solar power.

7. What is *Biodegradable?*
a. What happens when your Botox wears off.
b. When your child's grade in biology is lowered to an "F."
c. Mostly living things that can be broken down—by bacteria or other decomposers, like water or worms—into simpler substances.

8. What is a *Fossil Fuel?*
a. "Dino the Dinosaur's" gas station.
b. Your mother-in-law's cooking.
c. The remains of prehistoric plant and animal life that were buried beneath the earth's crust for millions of years and subsequently turned into coal, oil and natural gases that, when burned, provide energy.

9. What are *Carbon Credits?*
a. Pieces of coal that Santa delivers when you've been bad.
b. Prestigious black credit cards.
c. A system that has been created to reduce greenhouse gases on a huge scale by capping total annual industrial emissions and allowing companies to buy necessary credits from companies that have not used their allotment.

10. What is *Global Warming?*
a. All the world's baby boomers having hot flashes at the same time.
b. What happens to the world atlas that you left on the radiator.
c. An increase in the Earth's average temperature that often cause climatic changes.

11. What is *Organic?*

a. The really loud music played at a church service.
b. Your first party dress that was made from scratchy material.
c. Something (for example, food), which must be grown and processed without the use of antibiotics, synthetic hormones, artificial ingredients, preservatives, excessive processing or genetic engineering.

12. What is an *R-Value?*

a. Why rats and roaches always survive.
b. The name of the newest discount retailer.
c. A measurement of the resistance of a building's insulation to heat flow—the higher the R-value, the greater the insulating effectiveness.

13. What is *Carbon Dioxide?*

a. Cher's black hair dye.
b. What the dentist gives you so you don't feel any pain.
c. A colorless, odorless gas found in the air that is generally non-poisonous unless the Earth becomes overwhelmed with it, at which point it becomes harmful.

14. What is an *Ecological Footprint?*

a. What you'll find on biology lab floors after a class has walked *through* their experiments.
b. How we identify newborn babies.
c. A measurement of how much land and water a human population requires to produce the resources it consumes, including what it needs to absorb its wastes.

15. What is *Electronic Waste (E-Waste)?*

a. What your father thought about rock 'n' roll.
b. What happens when your expensive GPS system takes you in circles.
c. Any broken or unwanted electrical or electronic device.

E-waste represents 2 percent of America's trash in landfills, but it equals 70 percent of overall toxic waste!

16. What is the *Greenhouse Effect?*

a. Spending too much time smelling the roses.
b. When your contractor convinces you that "money is no object."
c. A natural phenomenon whereby certain gases (like carbon dioxide and methane) build up in the lower atmosphere and prevent heat from the Sun's rays from escaping into space.

F.Y.I.:

Scientists fear that increasing concentrations of greenhouse gases may increase the average global temperature and lead to changes in the Earth's climate and weather patterns.

17. What are *Kilowatt Hours (kWh)?*

a. How long it takes you to climb Mt. Kilimanjaro.
b. The time you spend waiting for your husband to mow the lawn.
c. A measurement of electrical power or natural gas use.

18. What are *Renewable Energy Resources?*

a. Cosmetic surgery.
b. Magazine subscriptions that never end.
c. Natural resources, such as wind, water, trees and sunlight, which we will, hopefully, never completely run out of but are being used faster than they can regenerate.

19. What are *Natural Foods?*

a. What nudists eat.
b. A meal for cannibals.
c. There is no legal definition as to what constitutes a "natural" food, however, the food industry uses the term "natural" to indicate that a food has been minimally processed and is preservative-free.

Natural foods can include *organic* foods, but not all natural foods are organic.

20. What is *Ozone?*

a. The place where Dorothy's house landed after the tornado.
b. Oprah's new parking space.
c. A gas that can be "good" or "bad" for the environment depending on its location in the atmosphere (which can be in the Earth's upper atmosphere or at ground level).

> **F.Y.I.:**
> At ground-level, "bad" ozone is an air pollutant that is harmful to breathe and damages crops, trees and other vegetation. It is also a main ingredient of urban smog. The level known as the troposphere extends about 6 miles up, where it meets the second layer, the stratosphere. The stratosphere contains the "good" ozone layer that extends upward from about 6 to 30 miles and protects life on earth from the sun's harmful ultraviolet (UV) rays.

Quiz Results:

This was not a pass/fail quiz. However, if any of your answers were not "c," you have serious issues that we are not equipped to deal with in this book. How well you did on this quiz is less important than what you plan on doing in your everyday life. Your ECHOes and your actions are what really matter.

> **F.Y.I.:**
> If you have a computer, the Environmental Protection Agency (EPA) has a great web site that lets you calculate an estimate of your personal (or your family's) greenhouse gas emissions. You can find it at http://www.epa.gov/climatechange/wycd/calculator/ind_calculator.html.
>
> Now take some action! While you're there, click on the "What You Can Do" section to find out how you and/or your family can lower your emissions while reducing your energy and waste disposal costs.
>
> For each action you choose to take, the calculator displays the amount of emissions you could avoid and how that amount relates to your total emissions.

Regardless of whether or not you refer to the EPA web site, I've pulled together a lot of ideas and suggestions that have been ECHOed to me. There are hundreds of things that you and your family can do, many of which will cost you nothing. Yet, almost all of them will save you money. Trust me—I'm a financial expert. Green is good—both ECOlogically and ECOnomically!

Chapter Three

ECO-ACTION—What You Can Do

Let's assume that money *is* an object, in which case you probably don't have the resources to completely redo, refit and replace everything in and around your house to bring it up to a "green standard." It is also likely that you don't have the luxury of going out and building a new ECOlogical trophy home.

Before you head for the hills or move back home with your parents (*gasp!*), there are things that you can do to reduce greenhouse gases and to save money. In fact, we have pages and pages of activities and tips.

Remember, our mission is to ECHO our findings with our children, schools, businesses, communities and, basically, anyone and everyone concerned with saving our world.

ECO-ACTION Family Meeting

What *is* an ECO-ACTION Family Meeting...and how does it work? Well, it's not a legislative body—a household is not a democracy, though it *can* and *should* encourage participation and respect among all family members. Ultimately, *you* make the decisions unless you have specifically agreed to a "majority rules binding vote." As far as I'm concerned, the adults are the CEOs of the home. As a CEO, it's up to you to encourage responsibility and be a model of positive behavior. This is, after all, the way the real world works. Like it or not, work isn't democratic either—it tends to be hierarchical—and this explanation may head off some gripes from your kids.

The ECO-ACTION Family Meeting will teach a wide variety of life skills based upon raising your kids' consciousness of the ECO-EFFECT. They'll learn and practice how to make decisions, set goals, research information, solve problems, negotiate, brainstorm, arbitrate, think creatively in a group, budget resources and speak in public. The Family Meeting can also help children understand the importance of respect when it comes to others' and their own ideas.

So, before you do anything else, I suggest that you call an ECO-ACTION Family Meeting to discuss what you hope to accomplish. Everyone should be included. No matter how young or old your family members are, it's important for all of you to be committed and to participate. If they can speak or listen, make them full-fledged participants in this Family Meeting.

The mission of your first ECO-ACTION Family Meeting is to create an ECO-ACTION Family Goal Statement. What do I mean? Well, you're going to sit there and write down specific goals that are going to be met and create an ECO-ACTION Plan describing how you're going to meet each goal. Then, you, as a family, will decide who is going to be responsible for each task.

A "Call to Order"

Make a set schedule for the Family Meeting, so that all family members can be present. Conduct it in a special place that feels somewhat formal because this is serious business–not just another dinner. Make sure everyone has their electronic devices turned off. Everyone needs to pay attention and take notes to share with the whole family. Remember, the agenda for this first ECO-ACTION Family Meeting includes the creation of your ECO-ACTION Family Goal Statement.

ECO-ACTION Family Goal Statement

Now that everyone understands the dynamics of the Family Meeting, it is time to proceed to your first mission, which is to set your Family Goal Statement. Simply put, this is a statement about who you are and what you stand for as a family, with regard to the ECO-EFFECT. Does this sound like a daunting task? Well, it isn't. Any *good* corporate mission or goal statement is simple. Yours could be something like:

"...Be the change we want to see in the world."
–Gandhi

"It's our world, and our family will help to take care of it."

"We will share our ECO-Actions with each other, the community and the world."

"We, as a family, are committed to using our money in the 'greenest' way possible."

Explain to your children that their Family Goal Statement represents a vision of what they want to create and make happen. Think of the ECO-ACTION Family Goal Statement in the same way that the people of the United States think about the Preamble to the U.S. Constitution:

"We the people of the United States, in Order to form a more perfect Union, establish Justice, insure domestic Tranquility, provide for the common defense, promote the general Welfare, and secure the Blessings of Liberty to ourselves and our Posterity, do ordain and establish this Constitution for the United States of America."

In other words, our Founding Fathers wanted to form a nation based upon fairness and peace. The Constitution that follows the Preamble contains the guiding principles with which to carry out this mission or goal statement.

Now, create your own ECO-ACTION Family Goal Statement. Once it is made, you can have the younger kids create and display an ECO-FRIENDLY wall hanging that illustrates your pledge or Goal.

Hint: Don't beat the Goal Statement to death. It doesn't have to be clever or zippy. It just needs to clearly state what you want to do as a family to make the world a better place—now and in the future.

Let's Step Back for a Moment

The ECO-EFFECT takes both ECOlogy and ECOnomics into account. Your home is the perfect starting point for both ECOlogical and ECOnomic lessons. Just as your ability to *EARN, SAVE, SPEND* and *SHARE* affects the ECOnomic cycle, your ability to reduce the use of fossil fuels, garbage production and pollution affects the ECOlogical cycle.

In other words, what happens in each and every home–multiplied by millions of households–affects the global ECOnomy as well as the global ECOlogy.

You are now going to create a working system based on your ECO-ACTION Family Goal Statement. You can't fix the problems before you know what's wrong. Even though we are raising our kids' consciousness to become responsible Citizens-of-the-World, we are starting this process at home–your home. Explain that one person...one home can make a difference and empower kids to ECHO to the world.

To make this system easier for everyone, we've come up with a methodology using terms that we've made up–*EEKs and EEPs*.

So, What's an EEK?

It's probably the sound you'd make if you saw the damage caused by an oil spill or a mouse in the kitchen. For the purpose of this book, however, it represents something that could be ECOlogically fixed or improved in your home or life. An EEK is also something you *are* or *should be* conscious of outside your house, an ECOlogical problem that you could help solve, instead of ignore.

What's an EEP?

An EEP is what we call an ECO-EFFECT POINT because the *point* is that we want you to be aware of doing something that makes an ECOlogical difference for the world. (It's also given when an EEK is fixed). In business, they use the term *carbon credit,* which is far too complicated for any mere mortal to truly understand or use. However, in your home, an EEP could be as simple as making sure the lights are all turned off when you leave a room, taping up your leaky windows, turning off the water when brushing your teeth or donating money to save the rainforests.

ECO-ACTION Detectives and Heroes

Now that you understand an EEK (something that needs to be fixed) and an EEP (what you're doing or have done to fix it), the next step is to transform your children (and yourselves) into ECO-ACTION Detectives. Together, you'll go through your house looking for things that need to be fixed, improved or replaced.

The idea is to keep in mind that what you and your family do to help ECOlogically improve your home will ECHO beyond your house–spreading to your community and even the world. Remember, the other side of the ECO-EFFECT is ECOnomics. Your ECOlogical "savings" will also translate into ECOnomic savings for your home, community and the world.

To make it even easier, we've created a series of charts that you can either copy or adapt for your own family's use. I consider them "training wheels for behavior." Just like my allowance charts (you can read about them in any of my money-related books) that outline individual chores, ECO-ACTION responsibilities will also become second nature after a while.

If your family is anything like mine, your little ones will be very excited about taking part in these new activities. On the other hand, your teenagers may exhibit typical teenage behavior, saying that everything you do is ridiculous and a source of embarrassment. You might hear, "I would rather eat dirt than do that!" As a parent, all you can do is stick to your value system and set the rules.

ECO-ACTION Citizen-of-the-World Chart

You and your children can now become ECO-ACTION Citizens-of-the-World and earn EEPs.

The activities that you and your children decide to tackle (based on EEKs) should be different from those they earn for their allowance. These jobs are done to help save the planet and, in the process, save you all money by reducing costs.

After an EEP is completed, make sure that the family member(s) who accomplished the goal, initial the chart. Celebrate the accomplishments with whatever you've determined makes ECOlogical and ECOnomic sense for your family. It should be something that you *all* agree on at an ECO-ACTION Family Meeting–just enjoy the financial savings, buy some of those washable, cloth shopping bags or a few energy-saving light bulbs...or you can even make a donation to an endangered species–just do something that makes everyone feel good, while making the world a better place.

If you refer to the ECO-ACTION Citizen-of-the-World Chart, the last column indicates who fixed the EEK and earned an EEP, meaning that they have contributed to making a difference. Remember, it's about awareness, not about quantifying everything.

Unlike carbon credits, you can't trade your EEPs to family offenders. Since the purpose of the ECO-EFFECT is to celebrate what you *are* doing and not to criticize what you are *not* doing–earning EEPs is a reason to celebrate.

ECO-ACTION
Citizen-of-the-World Chart

EEK (PROBLEM)	EEP (what should be done to fix it?)	ESTIMATED COST (To fix the EEK)	EEP DONE?	WHO DID THE EEP? (names or initials)
Front Window Leak	Caulk It	$3.50	✓	Gavin
Lights Left On	Turn Off Lights	N/A	✓	Naomi Mom Dad
Toilet Uses Too Much Water	Insert Your Bottle Invention (Ask your Kids.)	N/A	✓	Elijah
Old Light Bulbs	Install Energy-Saving Bulbs	$2.99 (prices vary depending on bulb size/type)	✓	Family

Find the EEKs

Remember, you can't fix the problem before you know it exists. In the chart below (or one like it), you and your family will record not only the problems, but also the estimated costs to repair, replace or fix them. Because ECOnomics is connected to ECOlogy, you'll want to demonstrate that there is a monetary value as well as an environmental value to your waste. The misuse of energy provides the most vivid illustration.

For example, there are certain bills–gas, oil, electricity, propane, water, etc.–that can be tracked. Sit down with your kids and show them your latest bills. Next, have them set up a chart that will measure month-to-month usage and costs for each account. Note: The savings will be part of their EEPs.

You and your ECO-ACTION Detectives have to find what needs to be fixed (like drafty windows or leaky pipes). Kids also have to research what it costs to make the needed repairs. This can be accomplished by using the Internet (with your permission, of course) or by talking to an expert at a local or national chain hardware store. They can even participate in your phone or in-person conversations with the repair specialist.

Citizen-of-the-Household Chart

These are unpaid chores that your youngest children–age 3 and older–do as "good" household members. These include personal duties like brushing teeth, picking up toys, going to bed on time, hanging up wet towels and helping unload the car whenever asked. Your older kids may need to be reminded of these responsibilities, but they certainly won't respond to receiving a "gold star" for brushing their teeth.

Work-for-Pay Chart

These are chores through which children learn the life skills necessary to run a home. Completion of these chores earns each child a weekly salary (an allowance) that is budgeted into four categories:

THE CHARITY JAR (10 percent to charity),
THE QUICK-CASH JAR (30 percent as "instant gratification" money),
THE MEDIUM-TERM SAVINGS JAR (30 percent for something more expensive) and
THE LONG-TERM SAVINGS JAR (30 percent for long-term savings and investing.)

ECO-ACTION Detective Chart—EEKS:

Location: *List by room or category*

EEK:	Estimated Cost:
What needs to be fixed?	(Cost per unit x units used = Your cost)

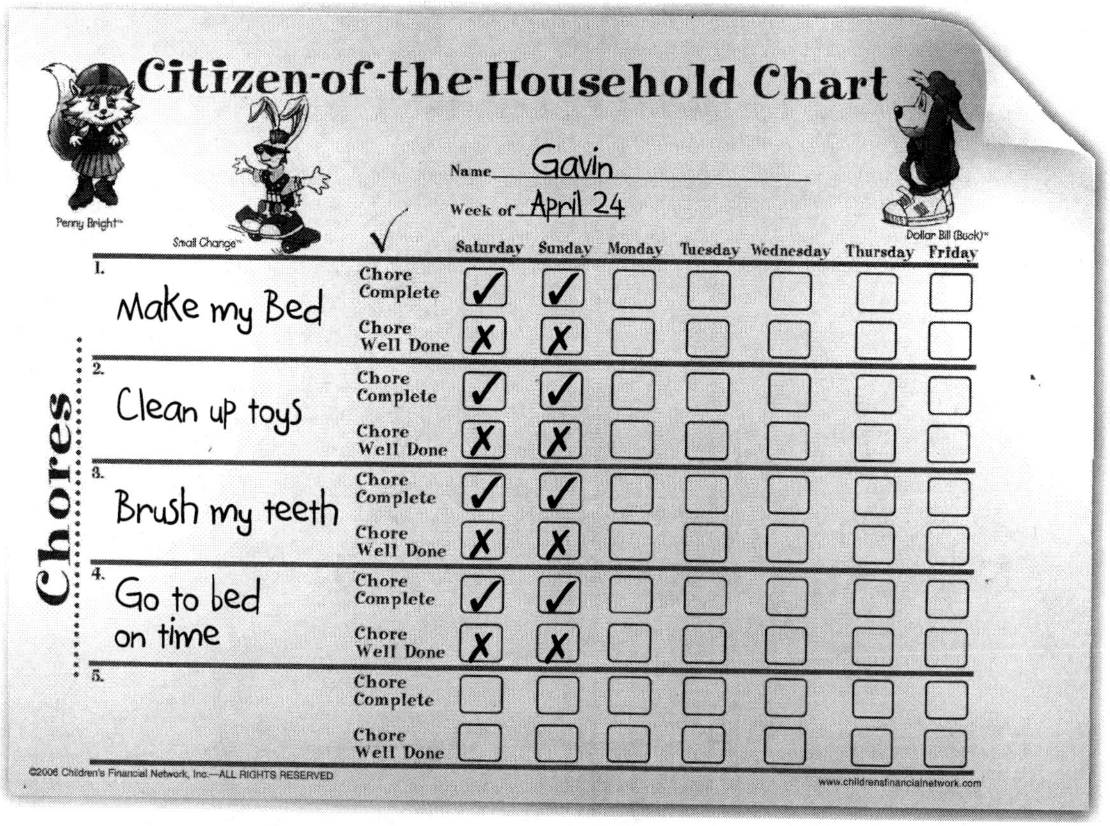

Citizen-of-the-Household Chart

Penny Bright™ Small Change™ Dollar Bill (Buck)™

Name Gavin

Week of April 24

Chores	✓	Saturday	Sunday	Monday	Tuesday	Wednesday	Thursday	Friday
1. Make my Bed	Chore Complete	✓	✓					
	Chore Well Done	X	X					
2. Clean up toys	Chore Complete	✓	✓					
	Chore Well Done	X	X					
3. Brush my teeth	Chore Complete	✓	✓					
	Chore Well Done	X	X					
4. Go to bed on time	Chore Complete	✓	✓					
	Chore Well Done	X	X					
5.	Chore Complete							
	Chore Well Done							

www.childrensfinancialnetwork.com

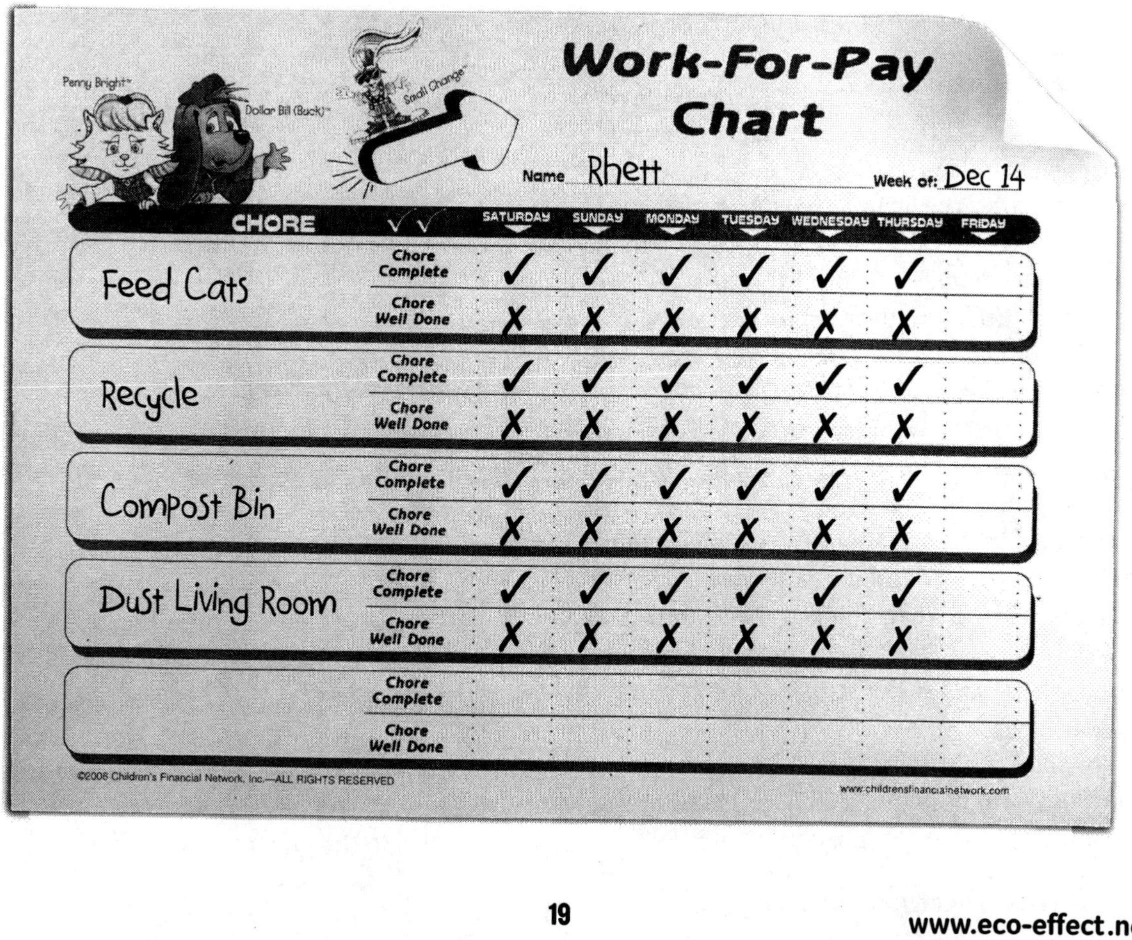

Work-For-Pay Chart

Penny Bright™ Dollar Bill (Buck)™ Small Change™

Name Rhett

Week of: Dec 14

CHORE	✓✓	SATURDAY	SUNDAY	MONDAY	TUESDAY	WEDNESDAY	THURSDAY	FRIDAY
Feed Cats	Chore Complete	✓	✓	✓	✓	✓	✓	
	Chore Well Done	X	X	X	X	X	X	
Recycle	Chore Complete	✓	✓	✓	✓	✓	✓	
	Chore Well Done	X	X	X	X	X	X	
Compost Bin	Chore Complete	✓	✓	✓	✓	✓	✓	
	Chore Well Done	X	X	X	X	X	X	
Dust Living Room	Chore Complete	✓	✓	✓	✓	✓	✓	
	Chore Well Done	X	X	X	X	X	X	
	Chore Complete							
	Chore Well Done							

www.childrensfinancialnetwork.com

Chapter Four

ECO-ACTION Detectives – Get Going

It really doesn't matter what you do to start saving the world, but it is important to just start doing something. You can start right now without even leaving the house. Did you know that, according to the EPA, your home produces more greenhouse gases than your car? So, let's begin by going through your home on a room by room or category basis, looking for things that you and your family can do that will contribute to a healthier planet, a healthier family and a healthier you. Speaking of health, we also hope your wallet becomes "healthier" in this process.

Perhaps before we start we should consider those things that affect the entire house–heating, cooling, electricity and water usage. It would be nice if money were no object and/or you were building your house from scratch. However, since most of us *already* live in our houses and *do* have limited funds to spend, let's consider what we can do *now*. Some of the changes are minor, while some are larger. Some might even be considered expensive now but will pay off in the not-too-distant future. Remember, it's getting started–doing *something*, even if it's just sharing this information with someone else–that will begin our ECO-EFFECT.

F.Y.I.:

As we write this book, the government and many utility companies are offering both tax credits and savings as incentives for using renewable energy and/or making energy-efficient upgrades. Check your energy supplier or go to www.energytaxincentives.org to see if you qualify for any of these offers.

It's time to turn into ECO-ACTION Detectives. You and your kids will search the house, garden, car, kitchen cabinets and refrigerators looking for EEKs. Can you imagine if everyone decided to join in this activity? The world would be a cleaner, healthier place to live–and that's the point!

Next, have someone create multiple copies of an EEK chart so that each room or problem area can be listed on one page. Eventually, you will take the results from each of these EEK charts and create the master ECO-ACTION Citizen-of-the-World Chart. All of these charts can be hand-drawn on paper grocery bags or printed on recycled paper.

Now we're going to go on an EEK journey that can

last for as long as it takes for you to search your home–weeks or months. As you collect the EEKs, incorporate them into the master ECO-ACTION Citizen-of-the-World Chart. Go room by room and then go outside. You and your family are opening your lives to an ECOlogical inspection. It's only natural to be embarrassed at the EEKs you find, but don't be upset–we *all* have EEKs.

Examples of EEKs your Detectives may discover:

ECO-ACTION Detective Chart—EEKs:

Location: *Whole House*

Lighting

EEK:	**Estimated Cost:**
Using old light bulbs	How many light bulbs can you afford to replace with energy efficient ones?
Lights left on in the kitchen	How much energy is used if the lights are left on all day? How much does the utility company charge you per unit of used energy? If the light is on for only a few hours, what can you save?

LIGHTING

Why It's Important to Fix These Kinds of EEKs, and What You Can Do.

Here is an example of what your children should be ECHOing to you or what you should be ECHOing to your children:

Change Five Lights

Change a light, and you help change the world. Replace the conventional bulbs in your five most frequently used light fixtures with bulbs that have the ENERGY STAR label, and you will help the environment while saving money on energy bills.

F.Y.I.:

According to the U.S. EPA - U.S. Department of Energy web site, "If every American home replaced just one light bulb with an ENERGY STAR qualified bulb, we would save enough energy to light more than 3 million homes for a year–and prevent greenhouse gases equivalent to the emissions of more than 800,000 cars."

ENERGY STAR is a joint program of the U.S. Environmental Protection Agency and the U.S. Department of Energy helping us save money and protect the environment through energy-efficient products and practices. The results are already adding up. Americans, with the help of ENERGY STAR, saved enough energy in 2007 alone to avoid greenhouse gas emissions equivalent to those from 27 million cars—all while saving $16 billion on their utility bills.

Other Lighting EEPs
Who Knew?

Much to my chagrin (since I grew up with the following belief), that there was a cost associated with the act of turning the lights on and off. There's only a cost if the lights are on.

Since lighting accounts for approximately 5 to 10 percent of the total energy used in an average house, consider the advantages of these energy-efficient alternatives or EEPs:

1. Use ENERGY STAR qualified compact fluorescent lights (CFLs). They use less than 25 percent of the electricity that standard bulbs use and last 10 times longer.

F.Y.I.:

It was ECHOed to us that if every home in New York City replaced 75 percent of their regular light bulbs with CFLs, we would save enough energy to run all the subways and light all the train stations—that would make it an extremely ECO-FRIENDLY city.

2. Shut off all the lights when you leave a room.
3. During the day, turn off lights near windows and let daylight do the work.
4. Instead of brightly lighting an entire room, focus the light only where you need it.
5. Keep bulbs and fixtures clean—dirty bulbs reduce available light and are a potential energy waster.
6. Replace light switches with dimmers or motion sensors (if you can afford them).
7. Use bright lights only where you read or work. Otherwise, use 25- or 40-watt bulbs. Three-way lamps make it easier to keep lighting low when brighter light isn't necessary.
8. Use night lights when a small amount of light is enough, like in a stairwell.
9. When you go away, use timers to turn your lights on and off.
10. If you can, use outdoor lights with a photocell and motion sensor so they go on only at night and when someone is present.
11. Instead of using dark lampshades and a high-wattage bulb to shine through, use a light-colored shade that can take a lower wattage bulb while still producing the same amount of light.

Here's Another List of EEKs for Your ECO-ACTION Detectives to Examine: Appliances

ECO-ACTION Detective Chart—EEK

Category: *Any Appliances*

EEK:	Estimated Cost:
Refrigerator half empty	Is it more efficient if it is full?
Stove's front burner doesn't work	How much would it cost to fix it?
Air Conditioners left running all day	How much could you save if it was only in use when you were home?
Iron left on	Are you wasting electricity?
Hair Dryer, do you need to use one?	How much energy does it cost to use one?

Why It's Important to Fix These Kinds of EEKs, and What You Can Do.

When buying new appliances or products for your home, look for ENERGY STAR qualified products to get the features and performance you want while helping to reduce greenhouse gas emissions and air pollution. ENERGY STAR qualified products and appliances will also save you money on your utility bills. You'll be surprised at how many products and appliances have earned the ENERGY STAR rating, so don't worry about not being able to find what you want.

Another EEK for Your Detectives: Heating and Cooling Systems

ECO-ACTION Detective Chart—EEKs:

Location: *Whole House*

Heating/Cooling Systems

EEK:	Estimated Cost:
Old Heating/Cooling system	How much would a new system or an upgrade cost? How long would it take for you to see a savings?
Old Filters	How much are new ones?

Why It's Important to Fix These Kinds of EEKs and What You Can Do.

Use Green Power

Green power is environmentally friendly electricity that is generated from renewable energy sources such as wind and the sun. There are two ways to use green power: You can ***buy*** green power, or you can modify your house to ***generate your own*** green power. Buying green power is easy (talk to your energy supplier about details), and it offers a number of ECOlogical and ECOnomic benefits versus conventional electricity, including lower greenhouse gas emissions, and increased clean energy supply. If you are interested, there are a number of steps you can take to create a greener home. For example, you can install solar panels and research incentives for renewable energy in your state.

Heat and Cool Efficiently

Simple steps like cleaning air filters regularly and having your heating and cooling equipment tuned annually by a licensed contractor can save energy and increase comfort at home while simultaneously reducing greenhouse gas emissions. When it's time to replace your old equipment, choose a high-efficiency model, and make sure it is properly sized and installed.

Heating and Cooling System—Earn EEPs:

According to Con Edison, here are some ways to increase the efficiency of your heating/cooling system while saving you money and reducing your home's contribution to climatic change.

1. Every fall, have your heating system cleaned and inspected by a qualified contractor. Have the same done to your cooling system every spring.
2. In the winter, set your thermostat to 65°F during the day and 55°F at night (and when you and the family go out). Each degree over 68 can increase the amount of energy you use for heating by 3 percent. That means, if it costs you $500 dollars per month to heat your home in the winter, a 3 percent savings is $15 per month–$180 total per year.
3. Instead of turning up the heat, wear a sweater and add a blanket. Keep a blanket in the TV room or any place in which you spend time. You're inactive while watching television or using the computer and, therefore, you may get colder. (I have ponchos and fleece jackets scattered throughout the house.)
4. If you can, install a programmable thermostat and program it to turn down the heat at night and when no one is home. Lowering the thermostat 10 to 15 degrees for eight hours a day can save you up to 15 percent a year or $75 on your heating bill.
5. Keep drapes or furniture away from radiators and baseboard heaters so heat can flow freely, and you can avoid a potential fire.
6. Remove air conditioners from windows when the weather gets cool. If you can't take them out of your window, you can enclose them with a cover and use masking tape to seal any possible air leaks.

7. Use an efficient humidifier to maintain comfortable humidity levels and help you conserve heat. Proper humidity helps you feel comfortable without turning up the thermostat. If you have an old-fashioned radiator, you can put a metal pan filled with water on top of it–creating humidity.

8. Use ceiling fans to circulate warm air in winter, especially in rooms with high ceilings.

9. On sunny days during winter months, open the curtains to let in the sun's heat and close them at night to keep in the heat. Note: Only open the curtains if your windows are well insulated. If your windows are not (yet) well-insulated, curtains can actually prevent drafts.

10. Close doors and warm-air vents in unused rooms, but, in extreme cold, be aware of water pipes that could freeze and burst. Place an inexpensive thermometer in your basement or near an outside wall that touches your garage and make sure that the temperature doesn't get close to freezing.

11. If you have a hot-water heating system, make it more efficient by releasing any trapped air from the radiators by turning the knobs at the radiator base.

12. Radiators can lose heat into exterior walls. Reduce this loss by placing reflectors between the wall and the radiator. You can find these at your local hardware store. They are inexpensive and easy to place between the radiator and the wall.

13. Keep warm-air vents clean. You can lift off the grating and clean what's right inside. I've been amazed how much cat hair and dust bunnies (which, in my house, are soft sculptures) I've found. You need a professional air-duct cleaning service to snake out and clean both the warm and cool air ducts. These service professionals should also inspect the air ducts to insure adequate air flow so there will be no heat/cooling loss. Often, there are listings of these professionals in the package of coupons most of us receive in our mail each month. If you live in an apartment, ask your superintendent if this is something that's done annually. If it is not, ECHO your suggestions to him or her.

14. Make sure that the professionals who come to clean or replace the filters for your hot-air furnace and heat-pump use the filters that last 6 to 12 months before needing replacement. Some filters need to be replaced every month during the heating season, which will cost you a whole lot more–especially if you have to hire someone to come in and do it.

15. Wrap any hot-air ducts that pass through unheated spaces with insulation. When hot air passes through a cold section of the duct, it cools and makes the whole heating system less efficient. This might be a great project you can do with your children.

16. Wrap hot-water pipes that pass through unheated spaces with insulation. For steam pipes, use non-foam insulation, since foam can melt. I've had my water pipes freeze in both my basement and garage, and believe me, it was not cause for celebration. Trust me, it's worth having a professional do the insulation work.

17. Here's an old-fashioned tip: Enjoy a hot cup of cocoa, tea or coffee to warm you up in the winter and a wonderful glass of cold water to cool you down in the summer. There's nothing better!

Air Conditioning–Earn EEPs:

According to Con Edison, doing some of these things could cut your cooling costs by 20 to 50 percent.

1. Every year, have a professional come in to inspect and clean your air conditioner or cooling system. A well-maintained unit uses less electricity.

2. If you have central air conditioning, keep the condenser unit's coils and fins clean. You may need a professional to do this. However, you can remove grass, leaves and other debris that may collect on or around the outside of the unit.

3. If you can, set your air conditioner to no cooler than 78° F. Setting your air conditioner lower than 78° F can increase your costs by up to 40 percent.

4. Don't air condition an empty room.

5. If you have central air, block the vents in unoccupied rooms. You can do this by simply taping cardboard over the vent.

Hint: If you don't want to repaint or repaper the wall, use masking tape.

6. Turn off your air conditioner when you leave home.
7. If you can afford it, install a programmable thermostat or use a timer to turn on your room air conditioner 30 minutes before you return home, rather than running it all day.
8. If you have central air conditioning, consider using a programmable thermostat.
9. During times of heavy usage, clean or replace air-conditioner filters at least once a month. Replacing an air-conditioning filter is so easy, my sister even takes hers into the shower and washes it while she's in there.
10. Instead of using air conditioning, use fans whenever possible. Fans use far less energy than air conditioners and often provide the same level of comfort.
11. Alternate the use of air conditioning and fans. When you're comfortable, shut down your air conditioner and turn on the fan. This approach can cut air conditioner use by up to 40 percent.
12. Shade windows that face south, east and west. Keeping windows, drapes and shades closed during the day helps keep unwanted heat out of your home, as approximately 40 percent of unwanted heat comes in through windows.

I'm Lost:

How do you know what's north, east, south and west? (Personally, I'm still working on "left" and "right.") Here's a great activity for you and the kids: If you have a compass, let them walk around the house and discover which windows face in what direction. If you don't have a compass, tell them that the sun rises in the east and sets in the west. They might be a bit grumpy having to get up before sunrise, but at least they'll discover for themselves which windows need to be shaded during the day.

13. Don't run your air conditioner when the outdoor temperature is below 70°F. Open the windows instead.
14. Install a whole-house fan in your attic to draw cool air inside through windows and force hot air out through attic vents. Note: This can be expensive since it's a huge fan that needs to be professionally installed, and they will probably have to cut a hole in your wall or roof.
15. When buying a room air conditioner, make sure it is the right size. The ENERGY STAR rating will recommend the correct unit for your room. A larger-than-needed air conditioner cycles on and off more frequently, reducing its efficiency. Frequent cycling makes indoor temperatures fluctuate more and creates a less comfortable environment.
16. Don't use the oven in the summer months—grill outside. It's time for family barbeques!
17. In the summer months, run your washing machine, dryer and dishwasher early in the day or at night, when it's generally cooler.
18. Install your air conditioner in a shady area, if possible.

F.Y.I.:

White roofs (literally, a shiny, plasticized white covering) reduce air-conditioning costs by 20 percent or more in hot, sunny weather. That means less energy is being consumed and fewer greenhouse gases are contributing to global warming.

Weatherizing—Earn EEPs

ECO-ACTION Detective Chart—EEKs:

Location: *Whole House*

EEK:	*Weatherizing* Estimated Cost:
Drafty Windows	How much would it cost to caulk/tape or replace?

Why It's Important to Fix This EEK, and What You Can Do.

Seal and Insulate Your Home

Sealing air leaks and adding more insulation to your home is a great do-it-yourself project. The biggest leaks are usually found in the attic and basement. If you are planning to replace windows, choose ENERGY STAR qualified windows for better performance. Seal and insulate any ducts in attics and crawlspaces to improve the energy efficiency of your home. Not sure where to begin? Check your phone book or your utility company to find a professional home-energy auditor who can also become an ECO-ACTION Detective and evaluate the overall energy efficiency of your home. Schedule the inspection during a time when your children will be home. Let them think of some questions to ask before the professional shows up. You'll find that most pros are happy to answer questions, especially those asked by children. As the professionals go through your home, they will recommend steps that you can take to eliminate drafts, keep your home more comfortable year round, save energy that would otherwise be wasted and reduce greenhouse gas emissions.

Weatherization

In order to conserve your household's energy, it is critically important to make sure that your house is as weatherized as it can be. If you can reduce escaping heat and air-conditioned air, you'll cut your heating and cooling costs by 15 to 30 percent, while also making your house more comfortable.

As we mentioned before, you could bring in an expert to do an audit or you can do it yourself. While you're at it, take notes so that you can decide what needs to be done and in what order. I'm assuming that you're on a budget like the rest of us, so do only those things that you can afford.

Inside—Out

First, check for indoor air leaks along the baseboard or flooring edges and at the wall and ceiling junctures. See if you can feel air flowing through these other slightly less obvious places:

- Electrical outlets
- Switch plates
- Window frames
- Baseboards
- Weather stripping around outside doors
- Fireplace dampers
- Attic hatches
- Wall—or window—mounted air conditioners

When you're checking your windows and doors, see if you can rattle them. If you can, that means air is possibly escaping. Have your kids ECHO with you about any ideas they might come up with to find air leaks. (They were given an exercise to do on their side of this book). Check your storm windows to make sure that they fit and aren't broken. You may decide to replace old windows and doors with newer, high-performance models. If that's too costly to do right now, then consider using low-cost plastic sheets over the windows. This is easy to do, and you can buy a kit in your local hardware store.

Outside—In

On the outside of your house, look at all the places where two different building materials meet, including:

- All exterior corners.
- Where siding and chimneys meet.
- Areas where the foundation and the bottom of exterior brick or siding meet.

Plug and caulk holes near faucets, pipes, electrical outlets and wiring. While you're outside being an ECO-ACTION Detective and inspecting, see if there are any cracks or holes in the mortar, foundation and siding. If there are any, then seal them with the appropriate material. Again, this may be a job for a professional, especially if the height of these EEKs is daunting. If you're going to attempt this EEP on your own, and if you're not sure what to use, then check with someone at your local hardware store. Make sure that your exterior storm and primary doors seal tightly and, if they don't, either replace them or add the appropriate sealing material, such as felt padding or caulking. For interior doors where there may be a draft, see if you can find some of those cute animal draft blockers that you can put right against the base of the door. You can even use rolled-up towels to do the same job.

Home Insulation—Earn EEPs

ECO-ACTION Detective Chart—EEKS:

Location: *Whole House*

Home Insulation

EEK:	**Estimated Cost:**
Old insulation	Does it need to be replaced? If so, what do you need and how much do materials and labor cost?

Why It's Important to Fix This EEK and What You Can Do.

Insulation

When your house was built, the builder probably used the amount of insulation that was recommended at the time. However, given today's energy prices—which seem to only be getting higher—the level of insulation used in your house now might not be enough, especially if you have an older house.

Check your attic hatch, as well as the entire attic, to make sure it's weather-stripped and tightly closed. If you've never been up in your attic, this may be a great adventure for you and your kids. There *is* a safety issue here—people have been known to fall through their ceilings. (I speak from personal experience.) While you're in the attic, make sure that openings for pipes, ductwork and chimneys are sealed. While you're up there, check to see if there is a vapor barrier under the attic insulation. Don't be scared, it could be tarpaper, kraft paper that's attached to the fiberglass batting or a plastic sheet. If you can't find a vapor barrier, consider painting the interior ceilings with vapor-barrier paint to reduce the amount of water vapor that can pass through the ceiling. Large amounts of moisture can not only reduce the effectiveness of the insulation but also promote structural damage–not to mention mildew.

Make sure that the attic vents aren't blocked by insulation and cover the entire attic floor with at least the current recommended amount of insulation, which you can buy at your local hardware store. To see how much you need, you can check this web site: www.eere.energy.gov/consumer/your_home/insulation_airsealing/index.cfm/mytopic=11350

Another issue about attics is that they become nesting areas for animals, birds and bats. As much as I love these creatures, "Mi casa is *not* su casa." They are not only a nuisance but they can also eat insulation, block the vents and create unwanted guano all over the place. They really do need to be removed.

Checking the walls' insulation is more complicated, and it might be worthwhile to have a professional come in and do a thermographic inspection to discover any leaks that need to be filled. Call a construction engineer or a contractor with expertise.

If you have a basement and it's unheated, check to see if there's insulation under the living area flooring. In most of this country, an R-value of 25 is recommended. Basically, an "R-Value" indicates insulation's resistance to heat flow. The higher the R-value, the greater the insulating effectiveness.

Remember the quiz and the R-value question? (You can go to the above web site to learn more about "R-values.")

The amount of insulation or R-value you'll need depends on such things as your climate, type of heating/cooling system and the section of the house that you plan to insulate.

In The Market for New Appliances?

Panasonic is a strong supporter of ENERGY STAR, with 335 products qualified to the standard. These appliances use less electricity and can lower your bills significantly. Some states may even grant rebates for families who purchase energy efficient appliances. To see if you qualify, visit: www.energysavers.gov/financial/70020.html

ENERGY STAR

Eco Effect
The Greening of Money

Chapter Five

The Bathroom—Singing in the Shower

Don't Let Money Go Down the Drain

ECO-ACTION Detective Chart—EEKS:

Location: *Bathroom*

EEK:	Estimated Cost:
Wasting Water: A leaky faucet	How much would it cost to have a plumber come in to fix or replace it? How much would you then save in water bills?
Using a natural sponge in tub	Is it worth taking this from the ocean floor or what does it cost to buy a washcloth?

Why It's Important to Fix These Kinds of EEKs and What Can You Do.

Saving water around the house is simple. Municipal water systems require a lot of energy to purify and distribute water to households, so saving water, especially hot water, can lower greenhouse gas emissions.

Four words sum up what you need to do in the bathroom: *Reduce your water consumption.* It may require breaking a few old habits like letting the water run when you brush your teeth and/or shave, or it might take a few little plumbing repairs like fixing those leaky faucets. (Did you know that just one drop every three seconds wastes 30 gallons of water a month? Get out the wrench!) Some EEPs are truly no-brainers. Here are a few quick bathing tips:

- Save water by taking fewer baths.
- When you do take baths, make sure that the bathroom door is closed so you won't have to add hot water because you're getting cold.

While you're looking at your plumbing, you should set your water heater no higher than 120°F or about midway between the low and medium settings. Also, wrap your hot-water storage tank with insulation, even if it's a newer model. If it's possible, insulate your hot water pipes, as well.

Showers

The biggest thing you can do is to take shorter showers using more efficient showerheads.

F.Y.I.:

Check out the ECO-friendly showerheads by Evolve at http://evolveshowerheads.com

Another tip is to turn off the water while you're lathering your shampoo and soaping up your body. Only have the water on to rinse yourself before and after cleansing. Don't leave the water running.

Showers account for nearly 25 percent of the water used inside an average house. A typical family of four, in which every member takes a five-minute shower every day, uses about 700 gallons of water a week. *If you have teenage girls, it's a lot longer.* You can easily cut that amount in half by using a "low-flow" showerhead. Not only are they inexpensive, but that same family of four will also save up to 20,000 gallons of water a week, as well as the energy that it took to heat the water. That, in turn, reduces the greenhouse gas emissions by more than 300 pounds per year and lowers the family's water and energy expenses. Talk about the ECO-EFFECT! Just be sure when you're changing plumbing fixtures that they have the EPA's WaterSense label.

An even cheaper option than a low-flow showerhead is to buy a faucet aerator that does the same thing. It mixes air into the water, resulting in a powerful stream that uses less water. Aerators cost less than $5, and all you have to do is screw them onto your faucet.

Another option is to have a plumber install a gadget that preheats your water. All you do is press a button near your shower, wait 30 seconds and then turn on a blast of instantly steaming water. This super invention saves between $160 to $200 a year and can easily be added to an existing home. It will pay for itself within three years.

F.Y.I.:

Check with your energy supplier—some of them, like National Grid offer significant rebates if you change to an "on demand" hot water system.

If you can't afford to have one of those systems installed now, you could have a contractor install a $30 heat trap that attaches to the pipe that leaves your water heater. It allows hot water to circulate through your tank when no one is using it (instead of letting it rise into the pipes, where it will eventually cool down and need to be reheated). A heat trap could reduce your annual water bill by 5 to 10 percent.

You can also get your kids involved and catch the running water in a bucket while you're waiting for it to reach the "right" temperature. Then they can use it to water the garden. Hopefully, when they read their side of the book they will be ECHOing their ideas to you.

Sink Faucets

In the United States, more than a trillion gallons of water are consumed through faucets every year. That represents more than 15 percent of indoor household water use. So, if you're out to save, consider either buying a high-efficiency bathroom sink faucet and accessories like aerators (that we mentioned above) that can help reduce consumption by more than 30 percent or install a sink faucet that's earned the WaterSense certification. By installing at least one WaterSense faucet or aerator in each home in the United States, we could reduce our annual water consumption by more than 60 billion gallons.

Sponges

If you think that buying a real sponge is a "good" thing, think again. They are natural products. However, when sponges are harvested, and you buy one, you are contributing to the stripping of nature from the ocean floor. You could use an artificial bath sponge since they are lovely but most of them contain polyurethane (not good). How about getting back to basics and just using a washcloth instead?

Toilet Paper

Buy recycled paper. You're only going to use it once before throwing it away, so it needn't be of the highest and softest quality. It may sound funny, but have everyone research the difference between recycled and non-recycled paper. My son and daughter committed whole-heartedly to recycled toilet paper, but it took a while to persuade me. I have since committed, as well, even though I'm convinced that I have calluses on my tush! In most instances, recycled paper is more expensive, so the purchase of this item could be discussed at an ECO-ACTION Family Meeting.

Toilets

Did you know that toilets use more water than anything else in your house? What's even more astounding is that while only 3 percent of the world's water is fresh, we in the U.S., flush more than 4.8 billion gallons of fresh water down the toilet every single day. That accounts for 9,000 gallons of water per person every year. Want to do something about it?

A cheap fix: If you have an old toilet, reduce its water capacity by filling one or more plastic bottles with water and placing them in the toilet's tank. You can also make sure that your toilet isn't leaking (you know it is if you still hear water running after you've flushed the toilet)—a running toilet tends to waste 200 gallons of water per day.

Another fix for an old toilet is to install an inexpensive flapper. The way it works is that it closes slightly early, giving enough time to flush out the waste but not the whole tank of water. You can even do it yourself.

An even better fix: Buy a high-efficiency toilet (HET) that produces the same flush with no trade-off in power. It can also reduce your household toilet water usage by about 60 percent each year, providing a significant savings on your water bill, which is something your kids could track.

You can do one better and buy a select-a-flush toilet. It's a two-flush system—one for liquids that uses only 1.1 gallons per flush and the other, for solids, uses the standard 1.6 gallons per flush.

If you want the *absolute best* ECO-toilet you can buy, in terms of saving water and energy, invest in a composting toilet, which requires little to no water. This toilet flushes waste into an odor-sealed chamber, where it then composts the waste into natural fertilizer. You empty it out two to three times per year and apply the contents directly to the soil. These magical machines are not only clean, safe and odor-free, but they'll also save you more than 40,000 gallons of water a year.

Towels

You can buy organic, unbleached cotton towels. If you use the smallest ones to get the job done, you should have less laundry to do (saving water and energy). In warm weather, consider air drying yourself and your towels.

Note: These towels are more expensive than the regular ones so see if they'll fit into your ECO-Budget.

Clean-up Naturally

Instead of using harsh chemicals, try using some of these mixtures that were ECHOed to us:

- All Purpose Cleaner
  4 tablespoons baking soda
  1 quart warm water

  To clean and deodorize surfaces, mix the ingredients and either spray or use a cloth to apply the solution. Rinse with clear water.

- Lime and Mineral Deposit Remover
  Soak some clean rags in vinegar, put them around the faucet deposits and then leave the cloth for an hour. When you return, you'll find that the deposits will have been softened enough for you to just wipe them away.

- Toilet Bowl Cleaner
  Sprinkle baking soda into the bowl, pour in some vinegar and then scour with a toilet brush. The combination both cleans and deodorizes.

Chapter Six

The Kitchen—Get Cooking

The Kitchen Awaits Your Touch:

ECO-ACTION Detective Chart—EEKS:

Location: kitchen

EEK:	Estimated Cost:
Food Waste	How much does uneaten food cost you?
Oven temperature not accurate	Do you need to replace a heating element or just buy a thermometer and make appropriate adjustments when you use the oven?
Running dishwasher half full	Figure out how much energy is used to run a load, how many loads do you wash in a week?

Usually one of the most frequented rooms in your house, the kitchen is not only a wonderful place to "be a family," it's also a place where ECOnomy really meets ECOlogy. There's food to be bought, stored, prepared and served. Then there's the cleaning and storage of leftovers...not to mention cleaning the room so it's free from harmful germs, chemicals and smells.

What's Important About These Kinds of EEKs and What You Can Do.

Food

Before we take over this room, let's consider what's in your refrigerator, freezer and cabinets. While we're at it, this is a great opportunity to involve your kids. Turn them into "Smart Kid Consumers" and have them go out and do a bit of supermarket research, reporting back to the family in one of your ECO-ACTION Family Meetings.

There are tons of conflicting articles on what is "good" and "bad" for us to eat. There is total confusion over the terms "organic" and "natural," and there is no *one* rule by which every family should live.

However, rather than do nothing, start by having someone volunteer to find out what the difference is between organic, natural or even genetically-modified foods. Then pick something that comes in all three varieties (for example, orange juice or eggs) and do a taste test. Everyone should taste the food and make a joint decision on which varieties will be bought on a regular basis. Don't forget that beyond taste, there's the contents...what's in the food? Read a few labels and find out what each ingredient is and whether or not you want to eat it. (Research the effect that growth hormones could have on animals and maybe even on humans). Some items should be non-negotiable. For example in my house, it's always *organic* eggs and milk. It may well be that some ECOlogically friendly foods may cost a bit (or a lot) more than their conventional counterparts, but the good that they do for you and/or the planet may be worth the investment. Some organic products may actually cost less, like "seconds" that you can buy at a farmers market. It's up to you and your family (as well as your finances) to see what works for you. Just keep at it and check out regular food purchases each week. Pretty soon, you'll all be much smarter and healthier shoppers.

Have you ever considered doing what many restaurants do? They recycle food by donating unsold meals to people who are hungry. This can be done through any number of charitable organizations. You can look at www.dccentralizedkitchen.org to see how people in the Washington, D.C. area are helping. If you live there, check out the web site and see if your family can help them make a difference. If you live in other areas, there may be similar groups already set up or maybe you and your family can think about setting one up.

"Waste Not, Want Not"

If we were able to reduce the amount of food that we throw away by just 25 grams (about the same weight as a slice of bread), we'd save 20 pounds of food each year—enough to make 16 meals. If all U.S. households did the same thing, the savings would be enough to provide three meals a day for a whole year to each of the 1.35 million homeless children in the United States. While we're on the topic of providing food for the homeless or hungry, next time you're in the supermarket, talk to the manager about having a local shelter come by right before the store closes to pick up leftover food (like from the salad bar) that might just be discarded.

Cooking

You can replace your appliances with ENERGY STAR qualified models. Also, before you start cooking with your new energy-efficient appliances, consider what the National Grid has to say about saving energy:

1. Cook with lids on your pots to contain the heat (energy), it will allow the water to heat faster.

2. If your gas burners have primarily yellow flames, gas is not burning effectively. If this is the case, call in your repair person or the gas company...do NOT play around with gas.

3. Use a separate oven thermometer to see if your oven has strayed from its temperature setting. If it has changed, use a thermometer when baking and roasting to figure out the real temperature.

4. Check the seal on the stove door for cracks or tears. If you find them, now might be a good time to replace the stove or at least the door, if possible.

Preheating Your Oven

In most instances, you don't really have to do it (popovers and soufflés not included!). But if you have to preheat the oven, don't do it for more than 10 minutes.

Did You Know?

If 30 percent of U.S. households used their oven just one hour less each year, we could save 60 million kilowatt-hours of energy—enough to bake a dozen cookies for every person in America.

Refrigerator

Of all the appliances in your kitchen, the refrigerator uses the most energy. You can't unplug it when you're not home but what you can do is keep it closed, clean and make sure the seals are tight. Bet you never realized that just door surfing...repeatedly opening and closing the door (hoping something delicious will appear?), adds $30 to $60 a year to an average yearly energy bill.

Did You Know?

1. If we all had more energy-efficient refrigerators and used them more carefully, we would save enough energy to light every house in the United States for more than four and a half months straight.
2. If we all turned our refrigerator's temperature up by only one degree, we would prevent almost 3 million tons of carbon dioxide from entering the atmosphere every year.

Besides keeping the door closed as much as possible, keep those condenser coils (on the bottom or back of the refrigerator) clean. Make it a twice a year chore and you'll find that the appliance will be less expensive to run.

Okay, it's expensive but a brand new energy-efficient refrigerator uses half as much energy as most that are 10 years old. If you can afford to buy one, you could reduce your refrigerator's electric bill by at least $60 a year for the next 18 years!

If you thought that keeping a spare refrigerator in the basement or garage was a good idea...think again. Storing those leftovers (from the year you got married) is probably costing you more than $150 a year. That one large one in the kitchen is actually less expensive to use, and more energy efficient to operate, than having two smaller ones.

Microwave Ovens

These are marvelously efficient inventions... especially if you keep yours clean. Consider this: If all of us in the United States cooked exclusively with a microwave instead of a standard oven for just one year, we'd save the same amount of energy that the entire continent of Africa consumes during that same year.

Stove/Oven

Want to do something small that can make a big difference? By using the right size pot for each burner, you could save $36 a year for an electric range or $18 for a gas range.

Did You Know?

Five percent of the energy bought and used per person in the U.S. is for preparing and cooking food. Over a year, this exceeds twice the energy a person in Africa used to power everything in his or her life.

While you're checking out your pots and pans, keep the glass and ceramic ones (can you part with the metal ones?). The former holds heat better, which means that you can turn down the temperature by about 25 degrees and the food will cook just as quickly.

When it comes to the oven, microwave or stove burner, keep them clean. Something as simple as that will allow you to cook faster and save money on your utility bill.

F.Y.I.:

Want a recipe for natural oven cleaner? Sprinkle some water on the oven surface, apply some baking soda and rub, using very fine steel wool. Wipe it all off with a damp cloth. Rinse well and dry.

Slightly more expensive than replacing your pots and pans, buy an oven with a convection setting—it cooks food about 25% faster (an internal fan circulates the hot air) and therefore saves energy and money.

No Peeking

If every oven owner in the U.S. opened the door one less time a year, we would prevent nearly 7,000 tons of carbon dioxide from entering the atmosphere each year.

When the time comes to replace your stove, spend a bit more and buy a self-cleaning oven. Since they are better insulated than regular ovens, it will take less time and energy to cook food. And, if you use the cleaning feature right after you bake something, you will use less energy to reach the cleaning temperature (about 850°F).

Trash Bags

Remember that discussion about paper or plastic bags in the grocery store? Well, if you decide to go with them instead of a washable, cloth bag, use them to line your small garbage cans, you'd not only save money (the average cost of 20 plastic kitchen bags is $5); but when one ton of plastic bags are reused, it's the equivalent to saving 11 barrels of oil. When one ton of paper bags are reused, up to 17 trees are spared.

Washing Dishes

First things first. If you use a dishwasher, forget about rinsing things before they go into the machine. Not only is it a waste of water but most of today's detergents (check out those that are "green") are created to clean the dirtiest dishes. However, before you just stick plates in the dishwasher, scrape off the big pieces of food and use the correct ones for composting (don't worry, we'll get to that soon).

Best way to lower your utility bill? Buy an Energy Star dishwasher. Short of that, run the machine only when it is full (you'll save 10 to 20 gallons of water a day). Dishwashers account for 15 percent of a household's water use, and heating the water uses hundreds of pounds of greenhouse gases. There's also nothing that requires you to use the dishwasher's drying cycle...how about letting your load air dry?

If you wash dishes by hand, you might not be saving as much money or water as you think. If the water's left running you're wasting more than 2.5 gallons of water per minute. How to solve the problem? Try washing and rinsing items together rather than separately. And, you can further reduce your water flow without changing the pressure by installing an inexpensive aerator or flow valve on your faucets.

Water Filters

Here's an idea that can save you money and help ECOlogically: Instead of buying bottled water, install water filters on your faucets. They can cost less than $30, or about a month's worth of bottled water if you drink a liter a day. If we all did that, we'd save enough plastic to make two water filters for every household on the planet.

ECO-ACTION Activity:

Be a Detective and find out what those numbers stand for on the bottom of plastic bottles. Hint: Perform a Google search with the question, "What do those numbers mean on plastic bottles?" Once you all know what they mean, you might want to buy or use different containers than you've been using.

Quick ECO Fixes:

- Cut down your use of plastic...for containers, for wrapping, and for chopping boards. Plastic is environmentally unfriendly both to produce and use.
- Say, "No" to foil...it's so thin that it has to go through many processes to be manufactured. That uses a great deal of energy; therefore, it comes at a high ECOlogical cost. If you must use foil, and it's not too disgusting, use it again.
- Invest in stainless steel or cast iron pots and pans instead of Teflon–or plastic-coated ones. The former might cost a bit more but they'll last longer and allow for more even heating. And, unlike other metals that can flake off and possibly cause health problems, iron is considered a healthy food additive rather than a harmful one.
- Slow can be good. A crock pot is extremely energy efficient (its electricity consumption is roughly the same as a light bulb) and since a meal can be cooked in one pot, it further reduces wasted energy when you cook food in separate pots and have to use water and soap to clean them.
- Instead of using traditional kitchen cloths, use a reusable e-cloth which is made from millions of tiny fibers with such a good natural cleaning effect that all you'll need to do is dampen it with water to clean grease, smears or grime. You can also buy simple organic cotton cloths in most grocery stores to use as dish towels for drying.

Back to Basics: Reuse, Recycle and Reduce Your Waste

If there is a recycling program in your community, then recycle your newspapers, beverage containers, paper and other goods. Use products in containers that can be recycled and items that can be repaired or reused. In addition, support recycling markets by buying products made from recycled materials. Reusing, recycling and reducing waste in your home helps conserve energy and reduces pollution and greenhouse gases from resource extraction, manufacturing and disposal.

Top 10 *Reasons* to Recycle

(According to the National Recycling Coalition)

1. **Good for Our Economy—**American companies rely on recycling programs to provide the raw materials they need to make new products.
2. **Creates Jobs—**Recycling in the United States is a $236 billion a year industry. More than 56,000 recycling enterprises employ 1.1 million workers nationwide.
3. **Reduces Waste—**It is said that the average person in the U.S. discards 6.5 pounds of garbage every day. Most of this garbage goes into landfills, where it's compacted and buried.
4. **Good for the Environment—**Recycling requires far less energy, uses fewer natural resources and keeps waste from piling up in landfills.
5. **Saves Energy—**Recycling offers significant energy savings over manufacturing with virgin materials.
6. **Preserves Landfill Space—**No one wants to live next door to a landfill.
7. **Prevents Global Warming—**In 2000, the recycling of solid waste prevented the release of 32.9 million metric tons of carbon equivalent (the unit of greenhouse gases) into the air.
8. **Reduces Water Pollution—**Making goods from recycled materials generates far less water pollution than manufacturing from virgin materials.
9. **Protects Wildlife—**Using recycled materials reduces the need to damage forests, wetlands, rivers and other places essential to wildlife.
10. **Creates New Demand—**Recycling and buying recycled products creates demand for more recycled products, thereby decreasing waste and helping our economy.

Top 10 *Things* to Recycle

(According to the National Recycling Coalition)

1. **Aluminum**
2. **Polyethylene Terephthalate (PET)** Plastic Bottles (Soft drinks and waters often come in these bottles, marked with the number 1 recycling symbol. They are approved by the U.S. FDA for consumer use. However, they are not made for repeated use, since they are difficult to clean.)
3. **Newspaper**
4. **Corrugated Cardboard**
5. **Steel Cans**
6. **High Density Polyethylene (HDPE)** Plastic Bottles (HDPE is used for milk and non-carbonated beverage bottles, and they are marked with the number 2 recycling symbol. In injection-molded tub form, HDPE is used to produce packaging for margarine, whipped toppings and deli foods.)
7. **Glass Containers**
8. **Magazines**
9. **Mixed Paper**
10. **Computers**

What Can I Do With My Old Electronics?

Properly recycling electronic waste (or e-waste) is one of the best ways you can help out the planet.

Your old TVs, computers and phones often contain toxic chemicals which can leech into the environment if not properly disposed of in factories and plants built for the job.

When done incorrectly, such as through open air burning, these chemicals can affect the water supply, land and people nearby. Panasonic and other companies offer take-back programs, free of charge, so you can be sure your old electronics are handled correctly. See www.panasonic.com/environment for recycling information.

Chapter Seven

The Living Room, Den and Bedrooms—Live it Up

ECO-ACTION Detective Chart—EEKs:

Location: *Living Room, Den and Bedrooms*

EEK:	Estimated Cost:
Unplug gadgets	How much electricity is being wasted on a daily or monthly basis?
Fireplace damper left open	How much energy can be saved by closing it when not in use?

Why It's Important to Fix These Kinds of EEKs and What You Can Do.

Let your ECO-ACTION Detectives get to work and go into their room (not as a punishment!) and after they've checked things out (and maybe even picked a few things off the floor and rediscovered that peanut butter sandwich that went missing weeks ago) let them run wild through the house checking to see if some, or all, of these things are done. (Be prepared for them letting you know just how ignorant you've been. Take heart; remember, "As your children get older, we parents get smarter." Bear with it; it's for a good cause). Here are some things that they (or you) can check out:

Gadgets

Make sure appliances are turned off instead of leaving them on stand-by, which can actually use almost as much energy as leaving them on.

Even better: Unplug appliances that are not hard to unplug after using them (like cell phone chargers) and if you're going to be away for any length of time, unplug everything that isn't essential (not the alarm system).

While you are at home, use power strips, which use a miniscule amount of energy when they're plugged in. For less than a $10 investment, you can save a bit of money by plugging your audio and video equipment into the power strip, and then switch it off at night. These strips also have the added benefit of protecting your equipment from power surges.

When you go to replace your TV, VCR or audio equipment, check the Energy Star rating. If the device is efficient, it will use 75% less energy when it's turned off than regular equipment. (The energy used when equipment is supposedly turned off is called standby power or phantom load.)

If you think you're saving energy and money when you buy equipment that uses battery power when it's turned off, you're wrong. Disposable batteries, for the most part, end up in landfills where they're crushed and release toxic metals into the air. Even if they're disposed of properly and end up in a hazardous waste center, their toxic metals must be separated out and stored forever!

F.Y.I.:

The electricity that you get from a battery is over 1,000 times more expensive than electricity from an outlet. If you must use batteries, use rechargeable ones.

Computer and Printers

Computers and monitors are second only to TVs in the use of energy by home electronic items.

Forget about using a screen saver. They don't save energy and were created to prevent monitor-burning (something that we no longer have to worry about with new computers). Better: When not in use either turn the computer off or put it into sleep or standby mode.

A typical home computer and printer consumes a lot of electricity each year. Cut the cost by plugging all your equipment into power strips and then turn them off when not in use.

Photocopiers use roughly the same amount of energy when in use as your dishwasher! They also use a lot of energy even in standby mode. The best way to save energy is to copy on both sides of the paper and do all your copying and printing at once so you can leave the machine off for the rest of the day.

Use less paper. It's the best thing you can do in your home office to save energy since it takes a lot to manufacture and transport paper to stores. What to do? Use smaller margins and typefaces; use recycled paper; print out final, not draft copies of documents; print on both sides of the paper; send e-mails or electronic faxes instead of paper letters and faxes whenever possible...you can even pay your bills and bank online.

F.Y.I.:

Con Edison even has an "Earth-Friendly Payment Plan." When you switch to e-billing, they donate $1 to a nonprofit tree planting fund. May not sound like much but they claim that "all by yourself, you can save 24 square feet of forest and prevent the release of 171 pounds of greenhouse gases simply by making the switch." Check to see if your local utility has a similar program.

Fireplaces

Keep your fireplace damper closed unless you have a fire burning. An open one can let 8% of the heat in your house escape...and in the summer, cool air escapes, as well. It can add up to about $100 a year NOT going up the chimney.

When using the fireplace, turn your furnace down to 55°F unless you have a new clean-burning, advanced combustion fireplace. Making a fire on a cold winter day almost always costs you more than using your heating system because a large amount of heat from your house goes up the chimney, causing your furnace to work harder to replace it.

Best idea: Seal up the damper and use your fireplace as a decoration.

Home Furnishings

Choose recycled fabrics for couches, drapes, chairs and other upholstery.

> **F.Y.I.:**
>
> If half of the polyester fabric made in the U.S. each year were produced with recycled materials, it would be enough to cover the entire state of N.Y.

One of the most environmentally friendly fabrics you can use on your floor is natural grass matting like sisal or jute, which is easy to produce, cheap to manufacture, is hardwearing and is totally biodegradable.

Instead of buying carpet made from synthetic fibers, choose one made from recycled materials. If you use 1,500 square feet, you could prevent the equivalent of more than eight thousand two-liter bottles from being hauled to landfills.

When it comes to cleaning your carpets, don't use vacuuming powder since it contains talc and chemicals that pollute the air. Use a water spray with a few drops of your favorite essential oil to freshen your carpets up instead.

When it comes to furniture, your best option is to buy used, refurbished or antique items. By doing that, you'll conserve manufacturing energy and materials and prevent vintage pieces from going into landfills. If you can't buy vintage furniture, try buying furniture that is made from sustainably produced materials such as plantation-grown lumber or wood certified by the Forest Stewardship Council. Try to avoid hardwoods like teak, mahogany, rosewood and hemlock... harvesting these species contributes to tropical deforestation, an annual loss of rain forest area larger than the state of Alabama.

When it comes to polishing your furniture, try this natural mixture instead of the usual store-bought sprays and polishes:

- 3 cups of olive oil
- 1 cup of vinegar
- Mix well. Apply to a clean, soft cloth and rub into the wood.

Chapter Eight

The Laundry Room—Clean It Up

ECO-ACTION Detective Chart—EEKS:

Location: *Laundry Room*

EEK:	Estimated Cost:
Using too much hot water	Can you do fewer washes with full loads? If so, how much would it save?
Running the dryer at top heat setting	What would you save if it was lowered or wash was hung out to air dry?

Why It's Important to Fix These Kinds of EEKs and What You Can Do.

You'll get more from less if you replace your old washer and dryer with new energy efficient machines (look for those Energy Star labels). Front loading machines are more expensive but the payback over time makes them more than worthwhile. Actually, it's said that your clothes will wash and dry faster with these machines.

F.Y.I.:

If the Laundromats and apartment buildings and dorms started switching to front-loaders, there would be a profound affect. There are thought to be approximately 40,000 coin-operated machines in the U.S. If just one load in every Laundromat, were washed by a front-load washer instead of a top-loader, we'd save 1 million gallons of water a day.

Whether you use a new or old machine...sort your laundry and wash it in the appropriate temperature. Some of us learn this lesson later than others. Growing up, Beth never knew that there was any other way to do the laundry than to dump everything in the machine, turn on the hot water and let that agitator go to work. Then she went to college and discovered that one could "sort" their clothes and did not have to worry about wearing either pink or grayish "whites." Anyway, the good news was that she did learn to use the warm rather than the hot water cycle.

Washing Machines

Forget the HOT button. If you use the warm wash and cold rinse cycles, you'll save 90% over the energy used when machine washing in just hot water. If all the households in the U.S. did this, we'd save the energy equivalent of one hundred thousand barrels of oil a day!

Dryers (Oh, hang it up)

Back to Beth again; what she neglected to do with water, her mother more than made up for in drying. It wasn't until her mom was in her 70s that she conceded to buying a dryer. Beth was one of the lucky kids who grew up with nice smelling, air-dried (but discolored) clothes.

So, the best thing you could do, and it's very inexpensive, is to use a clothesline when possible.

Clean your lint screen after each use and don't overload the machine. You could save up to 5% on your electricity bill. If everyone did it, we'd save the energy equivalent of 350 million gallons of gasoline each year.

Dry Cleaning (Okay, so you don't do it IN your house, but it fits in this section.)

If you must use dry cleaners, try to use them less often. Then, when you're there, request that they don't put your clothes in a plastic bag. Take things home in a reusable garment bag.

F.Y.I.:

If one in ten households took one less trip to the dry cleaners each year and did not use two plastic garment bags, the plastic saved could be stitched together to make more than nine thousand hot air balloons (not necessarily something you'd want...but it makes a point).

There are also ECO-friendly and organic dry cleaners... and wet cleaners who use biodegradable soap.

How Green is Your Cleaners?

Until there's a national standard and a truly green alternative to dry cleaning, your best bet might be to just not buy anything that says "Dry Clean Only." However, if that's not an option, The New York Times recently published a guide to Dry Cleaning Alternatives. They also suggested that you ask your cleaners which solvents they use for both dry and spot cleaning, how they dispose of hazardous waste, do they recycle hangers, use biodegradable plastic and packaging and use fuel-efficient vehicles to pick up and deliver the cleaning.

Eco Effect
The Greening of Money

Chapter Nine

ECO-ACTION in the Garden—Spruce It Up

ECO-ACTION Detective Chart—EEKS

Location: *Garden*

EEK:	Estimated Cost:
Polluting with Fertilizer	What are the costs of making your own ECO-Friendly fertilizer out of compost?
Planting non-native species of plants	Are they more expensive to buy than native plants? Are they a threat to your ECO-System?

Why It's Important to Fix These Kinds of EEKs and What You Can Do.

Composting

If, over the course of a year, everyone in the U.S. composted their kitchen scraps instead of tossing them in the garbage, the organic waste diverted from landfills could make a three-foot-high compost pile to cover the city of San Francisco. Okay, so we don't want to bury a city that I really love, but all that compost would make a super garden for, among other things, the lilacs that I do love. To find out how to make a composting area, you can go to www.howtocompost.org or any similar web site, and if you don't have access to a computer, there's plenty of information to be found at your local library or even a gardening center or club.

And, if you don't have the resources, space, time or interest in doing your own composting; go to www.stopwaste.org to find a group that would be happy to do it for you.

Not a "rotten" idea: Your kids should ECHO to you about composting.

Compost is organic "carbon based" material that breaks down (decomposes) over time to become nutrient-rich soil. Composting is fun and easy and your kids will ECHO the "Do's and Don'ts to you."

ECO-ACTION ACTIVITIES

There is so much for you and your ECO-ACTION Detectives to do right outside your door. And, they've been reading a lot about what they can do to make a difference on their side of this book. They can grow some of your food while helping to protect the environment. Here are some fun things that you can do together:

1. First things first, when you and your kids are outside, use a sunscreen to block UV rays and wear a hat and sunglasses. Eric, my dermatologist says, "Make sure it's at least 30 SPF."
2. Create a compost area and then use the compost as an organic fertilizer.
3. Instead of using a gas powered mower, get out that old manual one and while you're pushing it, think of the great exercise that you're getting. Your push mower doesn't consume any fossil fuels and doesn't emit any greenhouse gases. If you do use a power mower, make sure it is a mulching mower.
4. Plant organic or heirloom seeds and grow your own veggies.
5. Attract birds with a house of their own and you'll end up with a natural insecticide.
6. Fertilize and moisten soil by leaving the grass clippings on the lawn.
7. To control weed growth, use mulch.
8. Set up a rain barrel to catch water for your yard and remind the kids to schlep out the shower bucket and dump it on the lawn or garden.
9. Buy some ladybugs to control aphid populations.
10. Reuse empty containers for planting seeds.
11. Pull weeds (with their roots) by hand when the soil is moist (easier to do then, and you'll be more likely to get the entire root out, hopefully deterring future growth.)
12. Buy outdoor furniture that's made from recycled plastic.
13. If you build a deck, use sustainably grown wood.
14. For outdoor equipment, choose plantation-raised redwood or cedar (they are naturally rot resistant).
15. Opt for a play set that is made of nontoxic materials.
16. Start annuals from seed instead of buying flats at a nursery, it's cheaper. I start my seeds in planters in my house and then move them outside in May.
17. Don't plant edibles near chemically treated structures.
18. Treat swimming pools with a minimum amount of chlorine or explore saltwater or natural pools.
19. One of the best things you can do in your garden is to plant a fruit tree. Here in the northeast, apple, plum and pear trees are all hardy and will produce fruit as well as be a home for birds and other wildlife.
20. Go native by growing plants that are indigenous to your part of the country; they'll not only attract birds and butterflies but also save the time and expense of daily watering.

This is just the beginning of what can be done outside; put your heads together and I bet you can ECHO with your kids and the local garden center... or surf the Internet and come up with more ECO-Activities that you can do together.

Plant a Garden for Delicious, Healthy Eating

Get out there and plant a garden filled with vegetable and fruit seedlings. Not only will the activity be fun (okay, so weeding may not be up there with a spa treatment, but taking care of your own food can develop a sense of responsibility and pride). While your kids are out there working and reaping the results of their hard work–they are also working on reducing obesity (even if they don't know it). They're being active and they're growing healthier foods that they can cook and eat.

Do Your Homework

Before you do anything in or to your garden or yard, have the soil checked for everything from its acid and base content to its levels of possible contamination.

Remember that White House Garden? Great idea but no one thought to check for possible soil contamination. Turns out that there might be a high lead content due to sludge. Where did it come from? Don't ask. However, "The White House Kitchen Garden Team is committed to producing fresh, safe and healthy food as a learning opportunity about healthy eating, and they'll continue to do so."

If you can't grow a garden in your own backyard, check for one of over a million community gardens... you might be welcome to join in and help. And, even if you can't grow anything, at least become aware of what you're using when you prepare meals...see if you can replace processed foods with organic ones or at least try and get more fruits and vegetables into your meals.

City Greening

Branch Brook Park in Newark, New Jersey was the first county park to be opened to the public in the United States. After many years of use and mis-use, it was recently restored to its natural beauty with the efforts of some of the state's leading corporate and private donors who passionately cared about the city and its people. Among its champions are Pat Ryan and Prudential.

This program can be ECHOed throughout the U.S. and even the world... all it takes is time, effort and people who care.

F.Y.I.:

One final word; get used to a non-picture-perfect lawn. To become ECO-Friendly we will have to adjust our definition of "beauty." My lawn is now organic and guess what? There's moss, there are brown patches, grubs, weeds and even a few gopher holes...but it's real and it's beautiful and it's safe for all living beings (most importantly, for my granddaughter, Gavin).

Greening the Concrete Jungle

Part of ECO-Effect® is the e-forest program, which encourages kids to plant trees and take photos of them. The photos of kids and their trees are then uploaded to an interactive map on the ECO-Effect® website so other kids can become inspired and ECHO to their community about the importance of trees.

In cities, planting more trees helps reduce CO_2 concentrations and keeps the city much cooler in the hot summer months. Many people have even taken up rooftop gardening, which is a great way to insulate buildings, gain access to local produce, and make the concrete jungle a little more beautiful.

Look for opportunities in your area to plant trees or start gardens!

Eco Effect
The Greening of Money

Chapter Ten

ECO-ACTION in School—School Daze

Just as there are a million things you can do at home, there are just as many—if not more— when it comes to making your childrens' schools more ECOlogically friendly. We will be creating lessons for your kids to do at their school. Hopefully schools will be ECHOing within their communities, with businesses...with the world.

Energy costs are an enormous expense for our nation's schools. Out of this ECOnomic need to reduce costs and an ECOlogical need to green our world, The Green School Program was formed by The Alliance to Save Energy. This program engages students to create energy-saving activities in their schools by using hands-on, real world projects. They say that their "ECO-EFFECT" has been to reduce energy use by 5 to 15 percent in the participating schools.

Here's an example of what you and your children could ECHO to your school system... the Medford, New Jersey school district is reducing smog-forming emissions caused by school buses by changing from petroleum diesel fuel to an alternative fuel that is a mix of soy-based and petroleum diesel.

This school system went even further, in some schools they have been converting their natural gas boilers and chillers to geothermal systems which draw on the earth's inherent heating and cooling properties for climate control.

To conserve natural resources (and costs), they have also introduced waterless urinals (yup, they work and are sanitary) and "day lighting," where floor-to-ceiling windows infuse rooms with sunlight while reducing use of artificial lighting.

The next step this system hopes to finalize is a massive solar heating panel project in its middle school that will reduce demand for electricity.

F.Y.I.:

A perfect example of the ECO-EFFECT in practice is Byram Hills School District in Westchester, N.Y. Parents, teachers and students are all working together on sustainability. Parents have created and funded a Foundation that, among other things, has allowed teams of teachers to attend and design units of study that will help their students become responsible and proactive future citizens of a clean and healthy planet. And, the students present their findings and project activities on a special televised program featured on their school's cable channel.

At the same time, parents are encouraged to make meaningful changes toward sustainable practices. They work collaboratively with the schools' staff and students on school building-level initiatives; while also facilitating communication and collaboration between the school district, parents, residents and the town.

Some of the schools' goals are to improve bus ridership, start composting, create zero-waste lunches, plant a sustainable garden, adopt a street for clean-up and improve drinking container recycling.

According to the Foundation News (Fall 2008), "Not only does this ground-breaking project place Byram Hills on the cutting edge of environmental studies and community action for middle school children, it also provides a deeply meaningful academic forum for students to engage in...the ability to understand scientific debate and governmental response at the local, national and international levels."

Is Zero CO_2 Emissions A Real Possibility?

People and companies are certainly trying! Through new innovations in technology, such as solar panels and energy efficient appliances, reaching the goal of zero emissions is a lot closer than you may think.

Panasonic is attempting to create a zero-carbon lifestyle through our Create-Save-Store-Manage energy strategy for the home. By offering consumers ways to lower their household emissions and to create their own energy, Panasonic is among the companies who are at the forefront of making zero emissions a reality.

Go Government!

We're not there yet but as of the completion of this book, The Green Schools Act was passed by our House of Representatives (July 2009), by a vote of 250 to 164 and has been passed on to the Senate for approval. If it becomes law, this bill could supply our schools with approximately $20 billion in grants to help them become greener. The bill calls for schools to meet certain green building standards by becoming more energy efficient and by using more renewable resources.

We will see the ECO-EFFECT in action. By improving our schools with green practices and technology, we'll also be creating new jobs for the ECOnomy.

In the meantime, other states have not waited for the Federal Government to go green. In 2006, Michigan passed its "Michigan Green School Act." Their schools have to meet certain criteria to be designated as being "green," by making wise ECOlogical and energy-saving choices.

One of their schools, the Hartland High School, said that their participation in this program produced a savings of over $35,000 in energy costs.

Also, with the guidance of The Leadership in Energy and Environmental Design (LEED), green schools are being built from scratch around the country. Green schools cost less to operate and just think of the freed-up resources that can now go into our children's education!

If you look at the other side of this book, you'll notice a whole list of activities that your children can do and then ECHO to their teachers and classmates.

Let us hear your ECHO by emailing me at www.eco-effect.net and tell us what your school is doing for the ECO-EFFECT.

Go Communities!
Eco-Logical Communities

Communities are special entities encompassing government, school systems, business, non-profits, and faith groups. City governments often take the lead in promoting sustainability at the local level, bringing together all of the various elements that make up a functioning and thriving community. Environmental problems can seem overwhelming and individual effort can seem futile. But when an entire community engages in stewardship for their shared resources, the impossible becomes possible, and people are empowered to make a difference.

Today's cities need to be ECOnomically and ECOlogically savvy in order to be sustainable. Innovative cities can be found in all corners of the world and come in a variety of sizes. One such community is Fayetteville, Arkansas, where a community engagement program called Eco-Logical Communities was born. Eco-Logical Communities is based on the idea that what gets measured gets managed. At the program's core are three elements: a dashboard for environmental metrics, web-based tools that households, businesses, and others can use to reduce environmental impacts, and tools for engaging everyone in a community-wide campaign to steward local environmental resources. I am so thrilled that the ECO-EFFECT is their tool of choice for engaging that all important segment of their population: the children. The ECO-EFFECT book will be distributed to children in Fayetteville and will be used to teach children valuable lessons about ECOnomics and ECOlogy so they will "ECHO" to their parents and to their community!

PASS ON THE GIFT

HEIFER®

INTERNATIONAL

Moolah: Heifer International

A cow's contented moo echoes in the dark of an African night. Rain on a sturdy tin roof lulls a child to sleep in South America. Deep snows quiet a night in Eastern Europe as children sleep, their tummies full with warm milk.

All around the world, one good deed is echoed many times over as the work of Heifer International sounds out, loud and strong. Heifer International gives animals to poor families around the world and trains them in environmentally safe agriculture. These families continue the ECHO as they agree to "Pass on the Gift" of training and their animal's offspring to another family in need, creating an ever-widening circle of hope. That ECHO of one goat... one cow... one llama... one act... is how each one of us can make sustainable change in a world badly in need of it.

When you give a gift to Heifer International, you start a chain reaction of helping people stand strong on their own. You give people a way out, not a handout. If you look... and if you listen... you can hear the ECHO.

Heifer International's guiding philosophy is based on the old adage: Give people a fish and they eat today—teach them to fish and they eat for the rest of their lives. Heifer International gives animals to poor families around the world and trains them in environmentally safe agriculture. These families then agree to "Pass on the Gift" of their animal's offspring to another family in need in their community creating an ever-widening circle of hope. An ECO-EFFECT.

To trust that our lives have meaning, every one of us needs to effect some tangible change in the world. When so many people are out there, looking for a way to help themselves, can any of us turn away?

With a gift to Heifer, you say that, in this world, hunger and poverty are not destiny. You start a chain reaction of all the amazing things that happen when people realize they can stand strong on their own. Heifer families get food and income, and we all get a better world. And you discover the power to make lasting change happen.

ECHO to Heifer International at www.heifer.org.

Eco Effect
The Greening of Money

Chapter Eleven

Transportation—Get Moving

ECO-ACTION Detective Chart—EEKS:

Location: *Airplane*

EEK:	Estimated Cost:
Packing too much luggage	What is the cost per bag?
Flying instead of taking a bus or driving	How much money could be saved?

Why It's Important to Fix These Kinds of EEKs and What You Can Do.

The heavier the luggage, the heavier the plane, and the more fuel it takes to fly the plane.

Minimize ECOlogical impact: tread gently wherever you go and support ECO-friendly destinations. For your next vacation, perhaps consider doing volunteer work – it pays off in so many ways. Have your ECO-ACTION Detectives find some of these opportunities on the Internet or you can all speak with your travel agent. Habitat for Humanity is a great example. Among the many other resources you can investigate are:

www.GlobeAware.org
www.responsibletravel.com
www.GapAdventures.com/EcoTravel
www.ecoTrotters.com
www.abercrombiekent.com/philanthropy

If it's possible, give up the plane for a train. Did you know that a train can use up to 70% less energy and cause 85% less air pollution than a commercial jet?

No train? Try a bus. It's a cheaper, as well as greener, alternative to flying or driving. The average car in the U.S. releases about a pound of carbon dioxide for every mile that's driven.

ECO-ACTION Detective Chart—EEKS:

Location: *Your Car*

EEK:	Estimated Cost:
Using too much gasoline	Have your kids figure this out for your gasoline usage; here's an example: Consider that gas is $4.00 a gallon. If you have a 20 gallon tank, it costs $80 to fill that tank. If you use ½ a tank less per weekend that saves you about $2,000 a year!

Why It's Important to Fix This EEK and What You Can Do.

Gasoline is a huge polluter. If one 20-mile trip per week was cut out (by, let's say, combining errands, or having your kids carpool to activities) counting every registered vehicle in the U.S., 41 million fewer tons of greenhouse gases would be released into the air each year.

When you drive, each gallon of gas that you burn produces carbon dioxide. Depending on what kind of car you drive, you can easily generate the cars' weight in carbon dioxide each year.

Passenger vehicles cause almost a third of smog-forming emissions in the U.S. So, the more that you drive, the more the planet suffers. Try to get out of the car and walk, bike, carpool, or do something to reduce your carbon footprint...this will have both an ECOlogical and ECOnomic effect.

ECO-Driving

- If you can't buy an ECO-Friendly car right now, there are ways to cut down on your fuel consumption with your present vehicle.
- If you have to drive, pack light. Extra weight cuts fuel economy. And, don't think that putting your luggage on the roof will make it better.
- Save money; use the cheapest gas that your car's owner's manual suggests.
- Set the cruise control button to the legal speed limit and you'll find that you'll prevent unnecessary speed changes that waste gas (and avoid tickets—again another positive example of ECOnomic and ECOlogical effect!).
- Drive more slowly. Each 10 miles per hour faster, will reduce your fuel efficiency by between 15-20 percent.
- When buying a car, consider going hybrid or see if you can get by with an electric car or cart. The car manufacturers are also working on new, more energy efficient fuel cells.
- Keep whatever car you own well-maintained to maximize fuel efficiency.
- Keep your tires fully inflated. This could improve your gas mileage by as much as 3%. This will also help your tires last longer. If we look at the average American, who drives about 12,000 miles per year, this could save you about 16 gallons of gas annually, assuming that you're traveling 25 miles per hour and paying about $4 per gallon of gasoline. Sixteen gallons may not seem like a big deal. However, if all U.S. households did this, 1.6 billion gallons of gas would be saved, or approximately the total volume of ice cream produced in the U.S. each year.
- Carpool it. If the average commuter carpooled every day, each would save at least 500 gallons of gas a year or $2,000 a year, assuming gas is costing $4 per gallon. If commuters shared a ride to work, this could be equivalent to taking almost 68 million cars off the road, that's about four times the number of new cars sold in a good year in the U.S.

No Car Option

- Try to take public transportation. Not only will you save on gas, but you'll also save some of the time you spend in traffic jams—not to mention what you'll save on the use of fossil fuels. We spend approximately 36 hours per year in traffic jams (obviously, way more time is spent if you live in or around a major city)—that's almost a full week of work.
- Telecommute. Over 40 million people work from home—at least part time. Telecommuting could prevent more than 2 billion gallons of gas use a year.
- Bike It. If it's safe, encourage your older kids to ride their bikes to school. Only 2.5% of students who live within 2 miles of school get there on a bicycle. By not taking a bus or car, those 600,000 students are saving almost 100,000 gallons of gasoline—a day! At $4 a gallon, that's $400,000 a day in savings. Have your kids figure out what you could save if they rode their bikes more often.

F.Y.I.:

It started in Italy and now it's spreading worldwide. What? Walking to school with what they call a "driver." Every morning paid staff and family members lead students to school a la Pied Piper...kids join in all along the way. Since 2003, Lecco, Italy has eliminated 100,000 miles of car travel and thousands of tons of greenhouse gases.

Eco Effect
The Greening of Money

Chapter Twelve

Next Step—Back to the Future

Back to the ECO-ACTION Family Meeting—Review your EEK Charts.

Your ECO-ACTION Detectives have scoured your home, and frankly, your life and uncovered lots of EEKs. Great. Now, as a family, you have to sit down and discuss their findings. Before they decide to tear down your home and build a Bio-Dome, there has to be a reality check. Remember, that the ECO-EFFECT deals with both ECOlogy and ECOnomics, so you have to consider what is do-able within your budget. You need to celebrate what you can and *are* doing and not feel guilty about what you are not doing. Those are the rules.

The other purpose of this Family Meeting is for your ECO-ACTION Detectives to tell you "why" it is important to deal with each EEK. They actually need to research why it's important, the cost, and in lots of cases, the savings. Plus, they need to research what can be done.

After you as a family (with you as the CEO) have gone over your kids' lists of EEKs and equally important—the cost of them, it's time to remind your children of your ECO-ACTION Family Goal Statement. Go EEK by EEK and decide what is practical. You may be able to buy tape and seal up drafty windows, but buying new windows, at maybe thousands of dollars a piece, may not be in the budget. Ask the kids what they are willing to sacrifice? Maybe carpooling with friends, cutting out that extra movie night or having dinner out, will save $2,000 a year in expenses and that may mean that one or two windows can be replaced each year. It's now time to explain that "waste" not only creates damage to our ECOlogy, it has ECOnomic, and therefore, monetary consequences, as well.

At ECO-ACTION Family Meetings set the EEK goals that you will work on as you uncover them. Because ECOnomics is connected to ECOlogy, you want to demonstrate that there is a monetary value as well as an environmental value to your waste. The misuse of energy is the most vivid example.

You have already sat down with your kids and shown them your latest gas, electricity, water, propane, oil and gasoline bills, and have had them set up a chart measuring month to month usage and costs for each account. Explain that you just don't take great joy in "picking" on them to turn off the computer, lights or TV when they leave the room—it costs money and hurts the environment.

So, if your utility bills are too high, EEPs would be earned by agreeing to turn the thermostat down a few degrees in winter and up in summer. Have the kids go to the EPA web site and figure out what would be the best setting for your part of the world.

I suggest that while you're all together discussing what can and will be done, you make your "ECO-

ACTION—Citizen-of-the-World" chart based upon the EEKs that have been discovered and that you've agreed to work on together as family. You will add more EEKs as your ECO-ACTION Detectives find them. As you all work on EEPs, you'll be helping to save the planet and, in the process; hopefully saving money by reducing energy costs. This chart can be hand-drawn or computer-designed showing EEKs (what needs to be fixed) EEPs (what needs to be done to fix them), the associated costs, and the initials of the ECO-ACTION Hero (person or persons doing the EEP).

What happens when the bills start to go down? Celebrate your family's ECO-EFFECT and, if you want, put the savings toward fixing some of those EEKs.

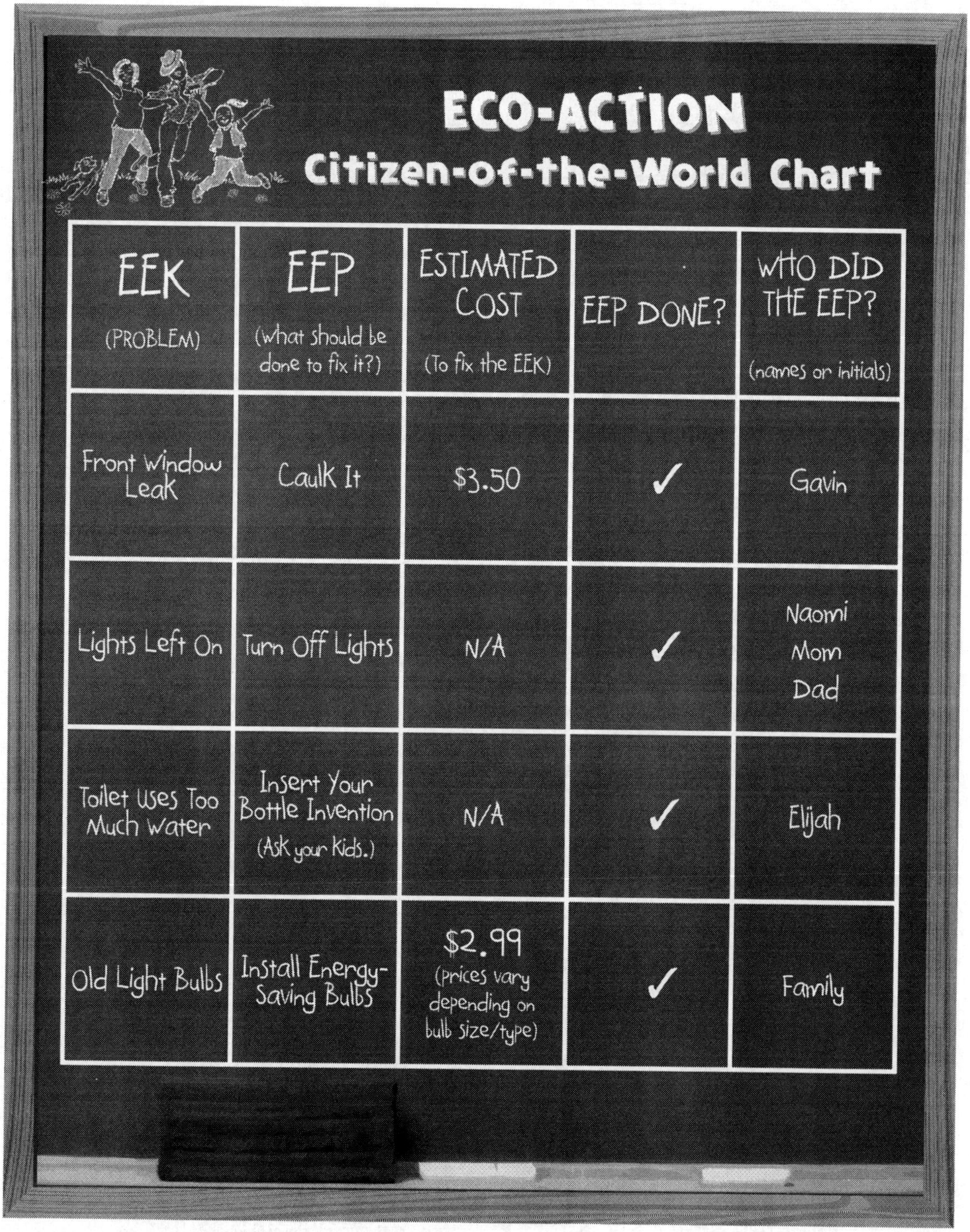
ECO-ACTION
Citizen-of-the-World Chart

EEK (PROBLEM)	EEP (what should be done to fix it?)	ESTIMATED COST (To fix the EEK)	EEP DONE?	WHO DID THE EEP? (names or initials)
Front Window Leak	Caulk It	$3.50	✓	Gavin
Lights Left On	Turn Off Lights	N/A	✓	Naomi Mom Dad
Toilet Uses Too Much Water	Insert Your Bottle Invention (Ask your Kids.)	N/A	✓	Elijah
Old Light Bulbs	Install Energy-Saving Bulbs	$2.99 (prices vary depending on bulb size/type)	✓	Family

Chapter Thirteen

The ECHO–Start Spreading the Word

You don't have to do the high kicks or be Frank Sinatra to "start spreading the word" about the ECO-EFFECT. We have created a way for your family to become more aware of the ECOnomic and ECOlogical consequences of their behavior. We hope that you've had some fun and will also save some money and the planet along the way.

The ECO-EFFECT is just a starting place for you and your family and we hope that you continue to ECHO from here on in. Hopefully, now you see the world in a whole new perspective. And, what may have been strange before will now have become second nature. As you have probably noticed, one person does make a difference, one family does make a difference and one community does make a difference. Can you imagine what the world would be like if everyone joined in? We have ECHOed to you—now, it's your turn to ECHO to your children. Start by handing them this book, so that they can read their side of it (peeking is allowed, even recommended). The next step is to encourage your offspring to ECHO with you and to you. Tell family and friends that energy efficiency is good for their wallets and good for the environment because it lowers greenhouse gas emissions and air pollution. ECHO to five of your friends and ask them to ECHO to five of their friends, and so on...together we can change the world.

All you have to do is take action and start doing something...anything...today. Sign on to saving the planet and not only will you feel good about doing the right thing, I bet you'll even save money in the process.

Remember, the ECO-EFFECT stands for ECOlogy and ECOnomics...make it work for you, your family and the world.

Now ECHO to your kids and "start spreading the word."

Sources That Have ECHOed to Us:

Books

Bennett, Clayton. *Green Your Home. Sustainable Options for Every System in Your House.* McGraw-Hill, 2008.

Brower, Michael and Warren Leon. *The Consumer's Guide to Effective Environmental Choices: Practical Advice from the Union of Concerned Scientists.* Three Rivers Press, 1999.

Brown, Lester R. *ECO-ECONOMY. Building an Economy for the Earth.* Earth Policy Institute ® W.W. Norton & Company, 2001.

Brown, Tom Jr.. *The Forgotten Wilderness.* The Berkley Publishing Group, 1987.

Brown, Tom Jr. and Judy Brown. *Nature and Survival for Children.* The Berkley Publishing Group, 1989.

David, Laurie. *The Solution is You. An Activist's Guide.* Speaker's Corner Books, 2008.

David, Laurie, and Cambria Gordon. *The Down-to-Earth Guide to Global Warming.* Orchard Books, 2007.

Editors of the *Green Guide* Magazine. *The Complete Reference for Consuming Wisely.* Natural Geographic, 2008.

Ellis, Brian "Fox." *Learning from the Land, Teaching Ecology Through Stories and Activities.* Teacher Ideas Press, 1997.

Fisher-McGarry, Julie. *Be the Change You Want to See in the World, 365 Things You Can Do for Yourself and Your Planet.* Conari Press, 2006.

Floyd, Esme. *1001 Little Ways to Save our Planet.* Carlton Books, 2007.

Gershon, David. *Journey for the Planet.* Empowerment Institute, 2007.

Gibbons, Gail. *Recycle!, A Handbook for Kids.* Little, Brown, and Company, 1992.

Gore, Al. *Earth in the Balance, Ecology and the Human Spirit.* Rodale Inc., 1992.

Green, Jen. *Why Should I Recycle?.* Hodder Wayland, 2002.

Hawken, Paul, Amory Lovins and Hunter L. Lovins. *Natural Capitalism, Creating the Next Industrial Revolution.* Back Bay Books, 1999.

Martin, Laura C. *Recycled Crafts Box.* Regent Publishing Services, 2003.

McDonough, Kim and Michael Braungart. *Cradle to Cradle.* North Point Press, 2002.

McKay, Kim and Jenny Bonnin. *True Green. 100 everyday ways you can contribute to a healthier planet.* National Geographic, 2007.

Rogers, Elizabeth and Thomas M. Kostigen. *The Green Book. The Everyday Guide to Saving the Planet One Simple Step at a Time.* Three Rivers Press, 2007.

Sterling, Mary Ellen. *Our Environment.* Teacher Created Resources, Inc., 1991.

Wines, Jacquie. *You Can Save the Planet, 50 Ways You Can Make a Difference.* Scholastic, 2008.

Zeiler, Freddi. *A Kid's Guide to Giving.* innovativeKids, 2006.

Magazines & Newspaper Articles

Baldwin, Teri. "Spring Cleaning" *North Fork Magazine*, April 2009.

Barranger, Felicity. "White Roofs Catch On as Energy Cost Cutters" *The New York Times*, July 30, 2009.

Bounds, Gwendolyn. "For a Green Thumb, Just Add Water" *The Wall Street Journal*, June 17, 2009.

Bounds, Gwendolyn. "Home Projects May Get Tax Credit" *The Wall Street Journal*, March 18, 2009.

Burros, Marian. "Obamas Prepare to Plant White House Vegetable Garden" *The New York Times*, March 19, 2009.

Fowler, Geoffrey A."Gadgets Show How Much Power Your House Eats" *The Wall Street Journal*, July 9, 2009.

Hackler, Jim. "The Power of 1" *Sky Magazine*, March 2008.

Hart, Sara. "Living Proof" *Continental.Com Magazine*, March 2009.

Higgins, Michelle. "Getaways That Are 'Guilt Free'" *The New York Times*, April 19, 2009.

Kuang, Cliff. "Burning Question," *Wired*, March 2009.

McCown, James. "Greener Good, Close-Knit Quarters" *Continental.Com Magazine*, March 2008.

McCown, James. "Greener Good, Seal and Wrap" *Continental.Com Magazine*, November 2008.

Miller, Peter. "Saving Energy: It Starts at Home" *National Geographic*, March 2009.

Navarro, Mireya. "Alternatives to Dry Cleaning" *The New York Times*, January 12, 2009.

Revkin, Andrew C. "Years Later, Climatologist Renews His Call for Action." *The New York Times*, June 23, 2008.

Rosenthal, Elisabeth. "In a City in Italy, the Schoolchildren Walk Where Once They Rode" *The New York Times*, March 27, 2009.

Scelfo, Julie. "New I.R.S. Incentives, From Cold to Hot" *The New York Times*, April 9, 2009.

Singer, Paola. "Gadgets Help Cut Energy Bills" *The Wall Street Journal*, July 8, 2009.

Zeller, Tom Jr., "Some Special Handling (of bulbs) Required" *The New York Times*, March 28, 2009.

"Earth Friendly Payment Plans" *ConEd Customer News*, March/April 2009.

"Paper, Plastic or Reusable?" and "Landfills Making the Grade." *ShopRite Earth 2008*, Volume 9, No. 1 – Spring/Summer.

Teen Side
Eco Effect™
The Greening of Money
Neale S. Godfrey
with Beth Polazzo
Visit our Web Site www.eco-effect.net

Table of Contents

About Neale

I've written 17 books for kids and parents, and I've created lessons that are used in and after school. I've been on *The Oprah Winfrey Show* 13 times helping families just like yours to learn about budgets and how to *EARN, SAVE, SPEND and SHARE* money. My kids think it's cool that I've even been a question on *Jeopardy!* and an answer in The New York Times crossword puzzle.

Now, instead of just talking about budgeting money, I want to talk about something just as big, if not bigger — the budgeting of our earth's resources.

How are they related? Well, no matter how much money you or your family earns, you've got to divide it up in order to spend or save for things that you need or want, right? In the same way, when it comes to the earth, we also need to save resources and "spend" them wisely.

This will not be easy. I'll be the first one to admit that I (and the rest of my generation) helped make a mess of this planet. What I'm asking you to do now is to join together so we can all help clean things up – both ECOlogically and ECOnomically.

www.eco-effect.net

The ECO-EFFECT
Why You?

Who says one person can't make a difference? Imagine yelling "Hello!" in a canyon. The sound of your voice would bounce off the canyon walls and then echo back to you, repeating "Hello, Hello, Hello." The same thing happens when you toss one stone into a pond and the ripples move out from where the rock has been tossed, making endless circles. One stone, one voice, one person can have an effect.

"ECHO...ECHO...ECHO"

Did you happen to notice the **ECO-EFFECT** logo on the cover of the book? Did you see the ripples/circles that surround the world? These represent all the **ECHOes** that will be created by you, your friends, your family, your school, your community, your country, your world. The hope is that, someday, there will be so many **ECHOes** that your **ECO-EFFECT** will have helped to make the world a better place. It's up to you to help make this happen. I know you can do it.

I'm challenging you to make an **ECHO** that resounds with good sense and that will truly bounce back and affect your family — and maybe even the world.

You're savvy, and I know that you have the ability to really make a difference. The world needs you and your generation...and we're asking you to start helping now. Pretty soon, you'll be inheriting the responsibility for taking care of the earth (and all the people, plants, animals and resources that exist). Then, it'll be up to all of you to leave the world a better place for the generations that come after yours.

Most of the generations who came before you didn't understand or care what they were doing to the Earth. I'm assuming that you do. I hope that this book helps you to understand why your role is so important and what you, your family and your friends can do to make a difference.

You can start right where you are...at home with your family. From there, you can let your actions ripple out to your friends, school and even the world. You are going to **ECHO** to others by sharing your smart **ECOlogical** and **ECOnomic** choices. While learning how to fix or change things yourself, you'll also be pointing things out to others in order to spread the word.

NOTE: If you don't know what some terms or phrases in the book mean, be sure to ask your parents or other adults for help. In return, be there to answer any of their questions. That is how the ECHO works.

I'm calling the choices that you and your family make the **"ECO-EFFECT."** If you flip this book over, you'll see that I'm asking the adults in your life to work and **ECHO** with you, and you should do the same with them. Together, you're going to look at things from both an **ECOnomic** and an **ECOlogical** point of view.

How? Well, for instance, before you buy anything from now on, I'd like you to consider two things:

1 **ECOnomy** — Is it a *need* or a *want?* You need food but you probably want "fast food," which comes wrapped in layers of packaging and probably isn't all that healthy, right? Think about how much extra stuff you buy and make sure that what you're purchasing is really worth your (or your parents') hard-earned money.

2 **ECOlogy** — What effect will your purchases have on you and the environment? From the example above, you can see that choosing "fast food" could have a more negative effect on both your health and the environment (in the form of disposable packaging).

Here are a few examples of how ECOnomy and ECOlogy are related:

- Although they might be a bit more expensive than non-organic foods, you and your family have the option to buy and eat organic foods that are grown and processed without pesticides and are said to be healthier for you and the environment.
- If you buy a better-made product, it will probably last longer, and you won't have to replace it quite as quickly. Also, it won't become "garbage" overnight. Obviously, that's as good for your wallet as it is for the environment.
- When you're in a store, look at the packaging — more is not better. It's simple — fewer layers of plastic and paper create less garbage. That means less has to be hauled away to landfills in trucks that use fossil fuels, such as gasoline. It sure helps save the environment, and it may even save you and your family money.

Eco-Action Activity:

Can You Come up with Other Examples of How ECOlogy and ECOnomics Are Related?

Getting Started ECO-IQ

Try asking some of these questions to your parents, teachers, coaches, after-school instructors or other adults in your life.

See how "green" they are!

1. **Of the 130 million cell phones that are discarded every year in the United States, how many are recycled?**
   a. 50% (65 million)
   b. 25% (32.5 million)
   c. 5% (6.5 million)

2. **Which refrigerator uses the most energy?**
   a. A full one
   b. An empty one
   c. A half-empty one

3. **The average person in the United States produces how many pounds of trash every day?**
   a. $6^1/2$ lbs.
   b. $1^1/2$ lbs.
   c. 10 lbs.

4. **How many trees are cut down every year to make disposable diapers?**
   a. 10,000
   b. 100,000
   c. 1,000,000

5. **The energy saved from recycling one glass bottle will light a 100-watt light bulb for:**
   a. 3 hours
   b. 4 hours
   c. 5 hours

6. **Each year, people in the United States throw away how many plastic straws and stirrers?**
   a. 138 thousand — enough to make a statue the size of The Statue of Liberty's torch
   b. 138 million — enough to make a statue the size of The Statue of Liberty
   c. 138 billion — enough to make a statue 20 times larger than The Statue of Liberty

7. **The people in the United States use 2.5 million plastic bottles every:**
   a. Year
   b. Week
   c. Hour

8. **If you stacked all the unrecycled aluminum cans (end-to-end) they would reach:**
   a. The moon
   b. Los Angeles from New York
   c. Mars

9. **What percentage of glass is recyclable?**
   a. 50%
   b. 75%
   c. 100%

10. **How many foam cups do people in the United States throw away each year?**
   a. 25 thousand
   b. 25 million
   c. 25 billion

11. **One tree can absorb the amount of carbon dioxide released by an average car that has been driven for:**
   a. 4,000 miles
   b. 400 miles
   c. 4 miles

12. **How many miles of gift wrap ribbon is thrown away each year in the United States? Hint: The amount is more than enough to tie a big bow around planet Earth.**
   a. 3,800
   b. 38,000
   c. 380,000

13. How many people in the world have running water?

a. 20%
b. 50%
c. 70%

14. Of all the piped water to your house, how much is flushed down the toilet?

a. 10%
b. 25%
c. 40%

15. Which state in the United States has the highest recycling rate?

a. New Hampshire
b. New Mexico
c. New Jersey

16. Every year, we make enough plastic film to shrink wrap:

a. A mile-long freight train
b. Texas
c. 25 football fields

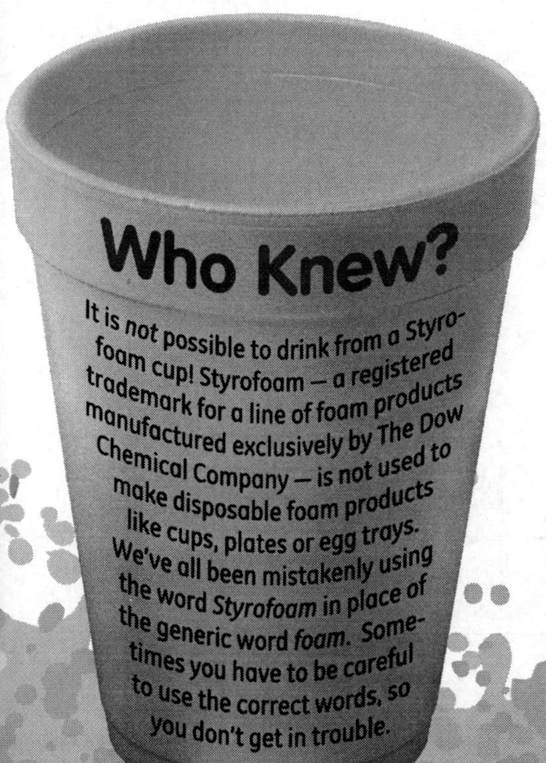

17. In the United States, enough plastic bottles are thrown away each year to circle the planet:

a. 4 times
b. 1 time
c. 10 times

18. How many trees' worth of paper, wood and other forestry products does the average person in the United States use per year?

a. 1
b. 7
c. 25

19. The amount of paper that is thrown away every year in the United States represents how many trees that had to be cut down?

a. 100 thousand
b. 1 million
c. 1 billion

20. The first recycling plant was built in New York City in:

a. 1798
b. 1898
c. 1998

Answers: 1: c, 2: c, 3: a, 4: c, 5: b, 6: c, 7: b, 8: a, 9: c, 10: c, 11: a, 12: b, 13:a, 14: c, 15:c, 16: b, 17: a, 18: b, 19: b, 20: b

ECO-ACTION What's the Problem?

"Global warming, the ozone hole, greenhouse gases, pollution, melting glaciers, polar bears going hungry"...you keep hearing really smart people (and some not-so-smart people) talking about these real or potential problems. Is it just adults complaining, or is it something about which you should worry? While we're at it, why is being "green" so important, and how does it affect you?

Well, it's important (and, yes, you should be concerned) because we all share the same planet, and, together, we are really messing it up. Too many people are making and consuming too much stuff. The stuff we make and don't reuse becomes garbage that eventually pollutes the air, soil and water that we all share.

ECO-ACTION CHALLENGE:

Can you think of any living thing that doesn't need air, soil and water in one way or another to survive?

We in the United States are the most to blame for messing up the planet. Did you know that the people who live here represent less than 5 percent of the world's population, yet we consume more than 25 percent of the Earth's energy resources?

Want to hear something else that's pretty shocking? If the rest of the world increased their consumption of stuff to U.S. levels, we'd need to create four more identical planets to supply all the necessary resources for everyone to survive...and that's just not possible!

How Did We Get into This Pickle?

Let's go way back to the way things were thousands of years ago when humans first made an appearance on Earth. Life was simple. These early people hunted animals for food and then used every uneaten part —bones were used for tools and weapons, and skins were used for clothing, warmth and shelter. Since no real garbage was produced, no real pollution was produced, either.

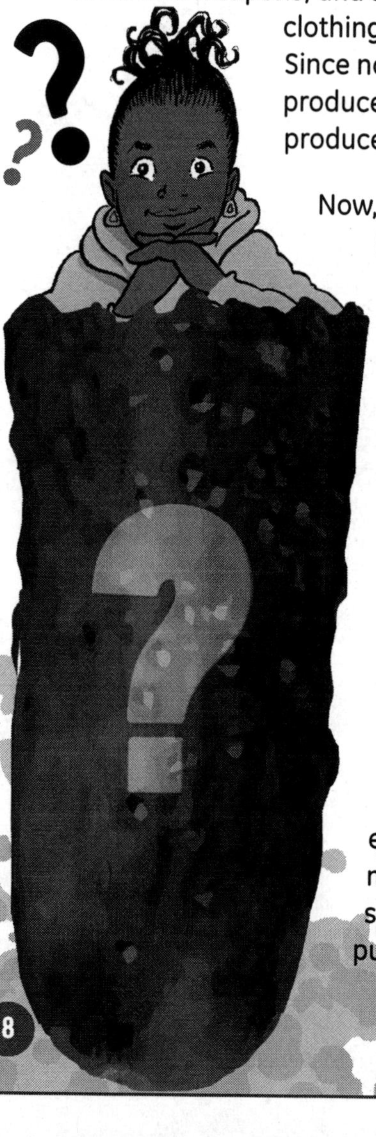

Now, fast forward to when humans first settled down and built homes. They began cooking in pots and eating from pottery. These clay pots eventually broke and were thrown away. As a result, what was created? Some of our first "garbage," that's what. This wasn't really "bad" garbage since it was biodegradable, which means it had the ability to break down harmlessly. Anyway, that early garbage gave our modern day archaeologists something to dig up and put back together in order

to explain how early people lived and worked. Archaeologists called this ancient garbage "artifacts" and put them in museums so that, today, you can see and understand what life was like thousands of years ago.

Fast forward to 5,000 years from now. What do you think future people (if there are any) will dig out of our garbage? Plastic water and soda bottles, batteries, aerosol cans, cars, cell phones?

WHAT ELSE? Make a list of five more things that you think people in the future will find in the garbage that we've left behind:

1. ______________________________

2. ______________________________

3. ______________________________

4. ______________________________

5. ______________________________

HOW HORRIBLE IS THIS?

There is even supposed to be an island of plastic bottles somewhere in the ocean. If you can find a picture on the Internet, send it to my Web site at www.eco-effect.net, and I'll post it and maybe even use it in my next ECO-EFFECT book.

ECO-ACTION Challenge:

Pretend that you're the archaeologist who has found your five items, and write a story about what you think you would say about our life (just like the archaeologists who found the clay pottery were able to piece together a story about how people lived in the past).

So, what will the people in the future say when they see our "artifacts" in the museums? How will they think we lived?

Well, the first thing they'll probably say is, "They sure made a lot of garbage!" After that, they might assume the following about people who lived in the past: (Remember, we're talking about us!)

- They invented lots of things in which to carry themselves and other stuff.
- They moved themselves by using cars, airplanes, trains, boats, trucks, golf carts, motorcycles and pogo sticks.
- They carried water in glass and plastic bottles.
- They packaged their food in cans and tins.
- They carried that food home in plastic and paper bags.
- They didn't like how they smelled, so they put deodorant in cans and sprayed it under their arms.
- They powered their homes and other things by electricity that was carried through wires covered in plastic.

I'm tired, but you get the point. We created a lot of non-biodegradable garbage!

We in the United States outdo the rest of the world when it comes to the production of garbage in the form of packaging — one out of every 3 pounds of our garbage comes from packaging. That adds up to 77 million tons of garbage — enough to fill the Louisiana Superdome in New Orleans 37 times! It's a vicious cycle. When the packaging is produced in factories, it causes pollution. We then purchase those packaged items. Next, after we open what we've purchased, we throw out the packaging, causing even more pollution!

So, what happens to our garbage when we throw it away? Where is *away*? Well, there is no *away* — it goes *somewhere*. The sanitation people pick it up and take it somewhere. *Somewhere* is a landfill.

WHAT IS A LANDFILL?

A landfill is a big hole in the ground where garbage is thrown. No big deal, right? WRONG, it's a very big deal. A lot of our modern garbage is made with chemicals that are toxic, which means it's poisonous. This poison can leak into the air in the form of gas, into the soil in the form of liquid, and even into the water supply, possibly poisoning or contaminating the water we drink. Not good!

Eco-EDEN The World in Perfect Harmony

When Earth was created, everything was, more or less, in balance. (I say *more* or *less* because no one knows for sure what it was like way back then.) Let's call that balanced environment "ECO-EDEN." There was no real garbage because anything that was left over (like animals or plants that had died and decayed) was absorbed into the land and air and was then used by new plants and animals. In fact, did you know that all of the water we have on the earth has always been here?

> **DID YOU KNOW?**
> Your body is made up of about 70 percent water, almost the same percentage of all the water on Earth (75 percent).

Water recycles itself. First, it evaporates into the air and then forms clouds. Next, it rains down to the earth—going into lakes, rivers and oceans. Finally, it is used by plants, animals, humans and even factories, and then it evaporates again.

Another example of **ECO-EDEN** is the way in which carbon dioxide (CO_2) works. When plants and animals die, they decompose. That decomposition releases CO_2 into the air. This gas is processed by living plants as a sort of food and helps them grow. Think of these plants as absorbing or breathing *in* the CO_2 and breathing *out* oxygen. Animals and humans, on the other hand, breathe *in* the oxygen that they need to live and breathe *out* the CO_2 that the plants use. This is an example of how plants, animals and humans were meant to live together in perfect balance—**ECO-EDEN**.

The earth, with all its living parts, was really good at absorbing CO_2, but it had its budget or limit. Today, the pollution that we create overloads the earth's ability to absorb CO_2. To make matters worse, we are destroying our rainforests and the plants that are great at using and absorbing the CO_2 as part of their lifecycle (which includes "exhaling" valuable oxygen). The balance between CO_2 and oxygen is off—too much CO_2 is being produced because of pollution. As a result, our **ECOlogical** budget (or **ECO–EDEN**) is out-of-whack.

Unbalanced Budgets

In my world of teaching the importance of making good financial choices, a perfect family budget is one that is balanced. In the **ECOnomic** world, that means that a family would spend and save the exact amount of money that they earn. If you spend more than you earn, your budget is out of balance, and you may go into debt to pay bills. That is an "unbalanced budget."

Just like what happens when we spend more than we make in a financial budget, we are now going into "debt" with our planet by producing too much pollution that can't be absorbed and recycled.

ECHO THIS WITH YOUR SCIENCE TEACHER:
I have a theory. I'm going to call it the "Let's Dig a Little Deeper Theory" or the "What Looks like Garbage, Smells like Garbage, Tastes like Garbage... Good Thing I Didn't Step in It Theory." My theory states that if the world were in perfect balance (think of ECO-EDEN), there would be a *natural* use for fossil fuels. In other words, all of those old, dead, squished plants and animals would have been "recycled" into new, alive, non-squished plants and animals. But *NO*, that didn't happen.

Fossil Fuels

Underneath the earth's crust, except in places like the La Brea Tar Pits (perform a Google search if you don't know what they are), you can find the transformed remains of ancient plants and animals that lived more than 300 million years ago. Those old, squished plants and animals seeped into crevices in the earth and, under heat and pressure, formed oil, coal and gas. In the past few hundred years, humans figured out that they could burn this muck, and it would give off light and heat. *Ta Da!* They began using it to heat homes, drive cars, fly airplanes, make foam cups, etc. As wonderful as that discovery was, it certainly has led to the continued downfall of **ECO-EDEN.** In fact, more than 85 percent of the energy that we use today is from that original dinosaur muck or, as the scientists call it, fossil fuel. So, dinosaurs were really important. If they didn't stomp around and get "knocked off," we'd never have a major fuel source today. Though, we also wouldn't have the pollution caused by it, either. Think about it.

(By the way, for all you scientists who are now rolling your eyes, there is no natural, earthly use for oil. **NOTE:** If you can tell me a natural use for fossil fuels, ECHO it to me on my Web site at www.eco-effect.net). If it looks like garbage, smells like garbage and tastes like garbage, therefore, it is garbage.

Eco-Action Activity:

Why do scientists give so many things really hard names to pronounce and spell, just like they did with the dinosaurs?

Come on, what's up with that? I would have named the Brontosaurus something simple like "Fred" or "Long-Skinny-Neck-Dinosaur." Here's a chance for you to rename five of your favorite dinosaurs:

1. Brontosaurus (*Apatosaurus*) = ______________________

2. Psittacosaurus = ______________________

3. Utahraptor = ______________________

4. Parasaurolophus = ______________________

5. Pentaceratops = ______________________

Greenhouse Effect/Global Warming – The Topic is Heating Up

In **ECO-EDEN**, there was another natural process that helped keep the world in perfect balance and harmony — the *Greenhouse Effect*.

You've all seen a greenhouse, right? It's a glass building in which it is warm enough for plants and flowers to grow — no matter what the weather is outside. The sun shines in through the glass and warms the interior of the greenhouse. The whole structure — the roof and walls — keep in the heat.

Acting just like the greenhouse, an invisible blanket of gases envelopes our planet. The sun shines through these gases, and a blanket of gas traps the heat, just like the glass that surrounds the greenhouse.

The good news is that this warmth permits us and all living things on the planet to survive.

The bad news is that the excess CO_2 we mentioned earlier just sits there like the glass on a greenhouse, unable to be used by plants and animals.

As the earth gets warmer, bad things happen – we call this process *Global Warming*. Each degree of heat makes a big difference. It doesn't seem like a big deal, but think about the ice cream in your freezer. At 32°F it's frozen, but at 33°F, just one degree more, it's mush!

Eco-Action Activity:

Make a list of five bad things that could and are happening to the earth as it gets too warm. I'll start you off: (Feel free to ECHO with your parents and teachers for help or ideas.)

1. Glaciers are melting
2. Sea levels are rising
3. ______________________
4. ______________________
5. ______________________

Bad Ozone – A Third Example of What Destroyed ECO-EDEN

What's ***ozone?*** It's a gas that exists way up in Earth's atmosphere, as well as at ground level. Here's the catch, just like CO_2, there can b[e "good] ozone" and "bad ozone," depending upon its location in the atmosphere.

When the layer closest to Earth, called the troposphere, contains ozone, it's the "bad ozone" and is considered pollution. It can ruin our lungs and damage trees and plants. The Los Angeles City Council may not like this, but when you visit their city or see pictures of it, you often see smog (bad ozone) and other bad stuff.

Smog A form of air pollution produced by the reaction of sunlight with hydrocarbons, nitrogen compounds and other gases primarily released in automobile exhaust. Smog is common in large urban areas, especially during hot, sunny weather, where it appears as a brownish haze that can irritate the eyes and lungs.

If you fly about 6 miles up from Earth, you will still be flying through the troposphere until you reach the next layer of the atmosphere, called the stratosphere.

Since you got to make up names for the five dinosaurs in the **ECO-ACTION** Activity, I'm making up names for the different levels of the Earth's atmosphere. Let's call the troposphere "**Claudia**," meaning "close to the Earth" and the stratosphere "**Wayne**," short for "way-far-away from the Earth."

We already know that it's bad when ozone mixes with **Claudia** because the pollution damages all living things. As we mentioned, though, **Wayne** starts 6 miles beyond Earth and then goes on for another 30 miles. "Good" ozone is produced naturally in the stratosphere. (Duh! I mean, in *Wayne*!) Here we go again, though. This good ozone is also being destroyed by the man-made chemicals used for the propellants in things like deodorant spray cans, fire extinguishers and spray pesticides. Refrigerant cooler is also a culprit. Take it from me, these are bad chemicals, and they're in a lot of stuff – destroying the good ozone.

When these terrible chemicals get into the air, they float way up high, stay around for a long time and eat away at the good ozone in **Wayne**. So, as the bad chemicals float up through **Claudia**, the sun's

rays cook them, and they release other deadly chemicals that destroy the good ozone in **Wayne**.

Why is that bad? Well, the good ozone layer in **Wayne** helps to keep the sun's harmful ultraviolet (UV) rays from reaching people and things on Earth. As more UV rays reach the earth, they burn humans, plants and animals. Too many UV rays can not only cause cataracts (a clouding of the eye's natural lens), but they can also cause cancer. In addition, UV rays can damage crops, marine life and a lot of other living things.

So, what are we doing about it? Well, for some people and living things, it's already too late to do anything. However, in an effort to try to make the situation better in the future, the United States and 180 other countries made deals with one another to stop making products with the bad, ozone-depleting chemicals. Warning labels must now be placed on certain products containing chlorofluorocarbons (CFCs), the bad chemicals. What's really scary, though, is that even if all the countries in the world stopped producing these ozone-depleting chemicals, the natural level of ozone in **Wayne** still won't return until year 2050.

Eco-Action Activity:
Go research other things found in nature that pollute.
Hint: mercury

Get Going Eco-Action Detectives

Okay, now its time for you to step in and become an ECO-ACTION Superhero...at least in your home, school and community. You know things are crummy, but you (and your family and friends) also have an idea (or two or a million) of actions that can be done to help make ECO-EDEN return. With this book, we're going to help you by giving you some clues about what you can fix or change by yourself and what you can ECHO to others, in order to make the world a better place.

Before you get to work, I'm suggesting that you and your family have a meeting to discuss your **ECO-ACTION** Goals. Talk about all the things that should be done and how much you think it will cost to do them. In lots of cases, you will find that you can help the environment and save money at the same time, creating a true **ECO-EFFECT**.

A Few Words about the Family Meeting

Your parents or other grown-ups in your life have also read about the Family Meeting on their side of the book. Here is the deal. Everyone gets a vote about what they want to do, but since your parents/guardians are the people who are responsible for you (and have the "big bucks"), ultimately, they get to decide what gets done. Is that fair? Maybe not, but that's the way it is until you have a place of your own and are running your own life.

ECO-ACTION Goal Statement

As a family, you all get to decide what your **ECO-ACTION** Goal or Mission will be. You need to spell it out. Think of it as a road map – unless you know where you're going, you won't know how to get there. It's the same way with a budget. If you have a goal, like saving for college or buying a home, you will be inspired to save for that, so you will figure out how to accomplish that goal. If not, the temptation to buy something else may seem more important than that distant goal.

I call it the **"Drip, Drip, Drip"** method of budgeting – a little money spent here and there. Each purchase is a drip but, just like the rain, each drip adds up to a puddle, a river or an ocean. Each dollar spent on something that doesn't help you reach your goal is a wasted resource. In the same way, each bottle tossed in the regular garbage or each window left open – when multiplied by thousands of people – is just like the **"Drip, Drip, Drip"** that adds up to energy wasted or more pollution, which equals a very **unECO-EFFECTIVE** world.

Family Goals

Here are a few examples of Family Goal Statements:

"Help to create a healthier world for all things."

"People messed up this planet, so we need to clean it up."

"We will make smart **ECOnomical** and **ECOlogical** decisions."

Now it's time to set your Family Goals. Your family can choose one from above or write your own. Make a poster illustrating your Family's Goal Statement (on recycled paper, of course) and hang it where everyone can see it in order to remind everyone why they are turning off lights, eating organic eggs or *not* buying a new gadget just because their friends have one.

Enter the World of EEKs *(not to be confused with the World of Geeks)*

Your next step, before you can fix or change something, is to figure out what needs to be fixed.

To help, I've set up a system called **EEKs**. What's an **EEK**? It's the sound you make when a mouse runs into the kitchen or, even worse, when you see someone wasting something they shouldn't, like clear, drinkable water when so many people in the world go thirsty.

We've asked your parents (or the adult reading the other side of this book) to help you go room by room to discover all the **EEKs** in your home – all the things that can be fixed or changed to make your environment and the world's environment more **ECO-FRIENDLY.**

You will now take on the assignment of becoming an **ECO-ACTION Detective.** You'll not only find the leaky faucets or drafty windows, but you'll also really see the link between **ECOlogy** and **ECOnomics** because you'll research the costs and savings to fix **EEKs**, as well.

You'll be doing all of this with an adult. You can look on their side of this book to see the sample charts you can make to keep track of your discoveries. Then, you can figure out the repair or replacement costs by using the Internet. By asking your parents if you can be there when they speak to the local plumber, electrician or handyperson, you'll be part of the **ECHO**.

To start discovering **EEKs**, you'll be doing **ECO-ACTION** Activities, going room by room. Here are a few things you can do:

See if air is leaking out of your house. It gets awfully expensive to either heat or cool your whole neighborhood. **So, here's the deal:** You're going to need a flashlight, pen and paper. We're just going to try this on the first floor of your house. (No Spider-Man tricks yet.) Wait until the sun sets and then turn off all the lights in the house. Give an adult a flashlight and send them outside. (How's that for a change?) Have them walk around the ground floor. They will turn the flashlight on and shine it around the door frames and windows. If you see the light where you are in the house, it is where it shouldn't be—you've found a leak! Keep track of where the leaks are and add the locations to a list of **EEKs** that need to be fixed. Then, I suggest that you let your parents back inside.

- **Why is it important to find the leaks?** Remember, if you don't know what the problem is, you can't fix it. Every draft wastes energy because you'll have to use more heat to keep your home warm. That means wasting more fossil fuels, not to mention wasting more money.

ECO-ACTION

- **Go to the attic to see if it's insulated. See if it looks old and cruddy. Ask your parents two questions:**

1. How long have they lived in this house?
2. Have they ever had the insulation inspected?

If the answer to the first question is "before you were born," and the answer to the second question is "no," you might want to **ECHO** to them by suggesting that they arrange an insulation inspection with an energy auditor. You can help them find this information on the Internet by performing a Google search with the phrase "energy audits." By the way, keep looking around the attic. You may find some rare treasures or real mice, in which case it would be fine to scream "**EEK!!**"

Eco-Action Activity:

Ask your parents if you can be there when the energy auditor comes. Make a list of questions you could ask. (Hint: Keep the ECO-EFFECT in mind. Ask how much energy could be saved. Also, ask how much things will cost, and what the estimated savings will be.)

- Put on your **ECO-ACTION Detective** hat again and go room by room, counting the number of light bulbs. (You may need to bring a pencil and notepad.) See how many of them could be replaced with energy-saving ones. (You can go to www.coned.com/kids or any other energy-based Web site to figure out how much energy you'd save by replacing the old bulbs.) Now is also the time to calculate how much it will cost to replace all those light bulbs with energy-saving ones. To do this, simply research the cost of the new bulbs and multiply that by the number you'll need. The cost will be high, but, remember, changing even one bulb will make a difference.

- Go around the house and unplug appliances that aren't in use – the computer, the printer, the coffee maker, etc. Leave things like the refrigerator, stove, washing machine and dishwasher plugged in. Let's put it this way, if you have any doubts about whether you should be unplugging something, ask first. We don't want you to get hurt or have a parent disown you. (Replacing all the food in the freezer is not a good thing, and it is also *not* **ECOnomically** smart.)

- Leaky faucets are annoying. That "drip, drip, drip" can really get on your nerves. What's worse is that it's not just water going down your drain; it's also your money going down right alongside it. Be an **ECO-ACTION** Hero and turn off faucets that are doing their own thing, or let your parents know that "Mission Control" has a problem. All you may need is a new washer, but even if a more complicated repair is needed, in the long run, it will be more **ECOnomical** than letting the faucet just keep on dripping. By the way, sticking something like chewing gum up the faucet to stop the dripping water is generally *not* a good idea. Believe me... scraping chewing gum out of faucets is a gross job.

Keeping Score Turning EEKs into EEPs

It could be as simple as making sure all the lights are turned off when you leave a room, taping up your leaky windows, turning off the water when you're brushing your teeth or donating money to save the rain forest.

You are not going to argue about who really turned off the light, as long as someone in the family has done it. This is not a blood sport or a reality TV show. It's a process of working together to make the world a better place.

In life, every big EEK deserves an EEP. What's an EEP? It's an ECO-EFFECT POINT that you earn for fixing an EEK. An EEP is earned for doing something that makes an environmental difference in your house, your garden, your school, community or even the world!

After your initial Family Meeting, have someone create an **ECO-ACTION** Citizen-of-the-World Chart (see on the right). Remember, you have been going room by room with your parents collecting a list of all the **EEKs** that need to dealt with. This **ECO-ACTION** Citizen-of-the-World Chart will indicate the **EEKs** (problems to be solved), the **EEPs** (what should be done to fix the **EEKs**), your research on the estimated costs, was the **EEP** done, and who did each **EEP**.

ECO-ACTION Rule: Celebrate what you and your family are doing to change the world!

EEK: *Something that needs to be fixed or changed to make the world a more ECOlogical and ECOnomical place.*

ECO-ACTION Citizen-of-the-World Chart

EEK (PROBLEM)	EEP (what should be done to fix it?)	ESTIMATED COST (To fix the EEK)	EEP DONE?	WHO DID THE EEP? (NAMES OR INITIALS)
Front Window Leak	Caulk It	$3.50	✓	Gavin
Lights Left On	Turn Off Lights	N/A*	✓	Naomi Mom Dad
Toilet Uses Too Much Water	Insert Your Bottle Invention (that you made after reading Chapter 8)	N/A*	✓	Elijah
Old Light Bulbs	Install Energy-Saving Bulbs	$2.99 (prices vary depending on bulb size/type)	✓	Family

** Note: It's hard to quantify the exact cost to fix some EEKs (like turning off lights).*

The next step is to decide how often you want to have a Family Meeting to review your progress. It could be weekly or monthly, but I don't suggest you go longer than that. Adults have a hard time remembering what they did *yesterday*. They'll never remember what they did and didn't do *months* ago. Trust me on this.

Track Savings

Since the **ECO-EFFECT** is about **ECOlogy** and **ECOnomics**, we're going to ask your parents' permission for you to keep track of the monthly utility bills. (That means all the energy, gas, propane and water bills.)

A kilowatt hour (kWh) is a word that you'll see on your parents' electric bill. It is a measurement to tell you how much power you are using and how much it costs. For example, if each kWh costs $0.124436 and you used 487 kilowatt hours, you'd multiply 487 X $0.124436, which equals a total monthly cost of $60.60.

Track the bills from month to month and then create your own chart. If you've all been doing your part and changing your ways (and light bulbs), you should see the bills start to come in with lower numbers. I can't tell you how gratifying this will be for your parents. It's also a terrific example of the **ECO-EFFECT!**

Let's Start in the Kitchen
A Rotten Idea

As you've gone room by room, no doubt the kitchen was a number one pit stop. It's usually the family meeting place and a great spot to begin being an ECO-ACTION Detective.

Here Are Some Major EEKs:

- Every year, each of us in the United States throws out about 1,200 pounds of garbage that we could compost. How much is that? A horse weighs about 1,200 pounds! If, for one year, everyone in the United States composted their kitchen scraps instead of scraping them into their garbage cans (only to end up in a landfill "somewhere") the organic waste (stuff that will decompose) could make a 3-foot-high compost heap large enough to cover the city of San Francisco.
- The United States is the #1 trash-producing country in the world, producing about 1,700 pounds per person each year. This means that 5 percent of the world's population creates 40 percent of the world's waste.
- At the rate we produce garbage, 500 new landfills are needed each year. Why? Most of the garbage that is dumped has not been separated into organic and inorganic stuff. The organic garbage needs water and air to decompose and because we pile the landfills so high and so tightly they never get a chance to complete this process.
- Bags that we only use once are a waste. They are either made from paper that comes from trees or from plastic that comes from fossil fuels. Any bags that are thrown away, cause more water and ground pollution...not to mention all the energy and resources it took to produce them.

Did You Know?

Plastic wrappers that end up in landfills may still be there 10-20 years later.

Eco-Action Activity:

Start recycling paper clips at home and at school and **ECHO** to your parents about their workplace. Enough paper clips are produced each year to hand every person in the world at least three.

Get Started on Those EEPs:

BE A "WRAP STAR"

To reduce some of that garbage and the creation of monumental landfills, here are a few ideas to turn some **EEKs** into **EEPs**:

- Instead of putting your school lunch in a paper bag that gets thrown away, pack it in reusable plastic containers. (There are ways to get these treasures without buying them. Whoever goes grocery shopping for your household might select food from the grocery store that's already in plastic containers or, if they order take-out food that is delivered, it often comes in plastic containers, as well.)

- Suggest that the grocery shopper in your house buys and then use cloth or recycled plastic bags instead of the disposable paper or plastic ones. Most grocery stores now sell them and some stores even give you a discount off your grocery bill if you use them. *Talk about the **ECO-EFFECT**.*

Note to Self: *Before those cloth bags look and smell like a science project gone amuck, wash them to get rid of the dirt and germs.*

You Are What You EEP!

Did you ever consider that an **EEK** might be something that you're actually eating?

Look at what goes into your mouth before it gets there. Have your fresh fruits and vegetables been sprayed with pesticides to keep bugs away ***(EEEK)***? Is there food dye in the processed food you're eating ***(EEEEK)***? Have the animals been given hormones or antibiotics, which end up in the meat that you are eating **(EEEEK)**?

During the summer, you can probably find local farmers who sell their produce at markets or farm stands. Their goods may be cheaper, fresher and more natural than those you could buy in the larger stores. You'll also be helping your local economy by shopping at these farm stands. This is an **ECOnomic** cycle, similar to the **ECO-EDEN** cycle. The money you give to local farmers goes into their pockets, and they, in turn, spend that money in your community on everything that they need or want. So, that means that the money has first moved from you to the farmer. Then it moved from the farmer to the stores, movies and other places in your neighborhood. See the **ECOnomic** cycle?

Slow Food USA

Slow Food USA is a national organization with local chapters throughout the country. Each chapter offers educational events and activities that promote sustainability and connects farmers, cooks, educators, students and everyone else who cares about their food and the environment. I met with students from The City University of New York (CUNY), and they started a composting project in some of their cafeterias as part of Slow Food USA. To learn more or to join your local chapter, visit Slow Food USA at www.slowfoodusa.org/.

"Go Organic"

If something that you're eating is *organic*, it means that it has been grown or raised without pesticides, hormones or dyes—closer to its natural state. It usually tastes better and is healthier for you and the planet. However, since it is more difficult and more expensive to grow and maintain organic fruits, vegetables, grains and meats, they are often more expensive to buy.

If your family decides to *"go organic,"* or at least *"partly-organic,"* then hold a Family Meeting to discuss ways in which you can afford it. Sometimes, this means cutting down expenses in other areas.

Eco-Action Activity:

When you're at the farmers market, ask a few of the farmers if they would answer some of these questions (and then think of some of your own):

1. How do you get rid of bugs?
2. How do you keep rabbits and other animals away?
3. What kind of fertilizer do you use?
4. Do you collect your own seeds or buy them?

Did You Know?

It is sometimes more expensive to grow and maintain **organic** foods? They are more natural, with fewer things added to them, right? It seems like this would make organic items **cheaper** and **easier** to produce, right? Unfortunately, though, this is not the case.

It is more **difficult** to grow organic fruits and vegetables because no pesticides are used. That means there's more of a chance that these goodies will be devoured by beasties. Also, because no preservatives are used, organic produce has a much shorter shelf-life and needs to be grown and sold much faster. Make sense?

For example, **ECHO** to the adults who live with you that if they could bring their coffee to work each morning in a thermos, rather than spend, for instance, $5.00 a day on fancy coffee bought at a coffee shop, it could really add up. Check it out:

IT ALL ADDS UP

Instead of Spending:
$5.00 a day on coffee X 5 days a week = $ 25.00

You Could Buy:
1 dozen organic eggs .... $ 4.50
½ gal. organic milk .... $ 3.50
Organic cheese .... $ 6.00
Organic veggies and fruits........................ $ 11.00
Total= $ 25.00

You and your family can make a list of other money-saving ideas that could be used to pay for organic food and recycled paper products.

Here are two ideas to get you started:

- Carry a refillable water bottle and stop buying expensive, disposable water bottles. Potential savings could be:
  2 bottles a day
  @ $2.00 each X 7 days = $28.00 a week
- Instead of going to a theater to watch a movie or to a restaurant to eat dinner, check a video out of the library and make a pizza at home. The following is an example of potential savings for a family of four:

ADD:
Movie tickets @ $7.00 each X 4 family members = $ 28.00
Meal out @ $15.00 each X 4 family members + $ 60.00
Total cost = $ 88.00

SUBTRACT:
Cost of homemade pizza ($20.00)
Free movie - ($0.00)
TOTAL SAVINGS = $68.00

Also, if you have been tracking the monthly savings from turning down the thermostat and turning off lights and appliances, you should find that there is some extra money in the budget. Then, perhaps at a Family Meeting, you might all agree to allow half or a quarter of the monthly savings to go toward **EEPs** such as buying organic food, recycled paper products or energy-saving light bulbs. By doing so, you will start to make a difference for yourself, your family and the earth. Congratulations, you will have become an **ECO-ACTION** Hero!

More EEPs: The Really Rotten Idea—Composting

Remember how much food is going to waste in those landfills? Here's a nifty solution to that **EEK**.

- Instead of throwing away your uneaten food (which gets sent to landfills, mixes with toxic garbage and doesn't decompose properly because it's not separated), you will create your own compost to be used in your garden, the woods or a city garden.
- Get a small, recycled steel can or bucket (with a tight lid) that you'll keep in your kitchen. Put it next to the sink or existing trash can. Instead of throwing leftovers into the regular kitchen trash can, you'll now scrape them into your new compost can/bucket. This will soon become second nature to you and your family, but, in the beginning, you'll need some practice before it becomes a habit. (Some habits are good!)

Did You Know?

It takes 75 percent less energy to make one can made of steel than one made of iron. If we recycled all our steel each year, it would save the same amount of electricity that is used in 18 million homes.

- If you live in the country or suburbs, and your family owns at least a small area of land, you can create your own compost pile of food garbage outside. If you're a "city kid" and don't have anywhere to create a compost pile, you can make a compost bucket.

Note to Self: If you are making a compost bucket, you'll have to add your own worms. Adults may not be thrilled about having a compost bucket in the first place, so you might not want to call it a "worm bucket."

Make a list of **DOs** and **DON'Ts** and post it on the top of your compost can/bucket to gently remind everyone of what *should* and *should* NOT be put into it:

DOS:

Veggies
Fruits
Tea bags
Coffee grounds
Newspaper (cut-up)
Cardboard (cut-up)
Egg shells
Napkins

DON'TS:

Meat
Fish
Metal
Glass
Rubber
Gum
Colored paper
Cheese

Who Knew?

Your compost pile will be healthier for you and the world if you are composting organic or natural things as opposed to those that include chemicals, fertilizers or other bad stuff.

Create Your Own Compost Heap

- Ask your parents to help you find a sunny spot in your yard. (Organic garbage decomposes faster in a warm spot.)
  HINT: They may not appreciate having the heap right next to the front door. Also, check out the distance from your kitchen. You don't want to have to "schlep" that compost bucket too far.
- There are different types of compost bins that can be bought or constructed but most of them are made from old wooden pallets and mesh wire.
- How big should it be? They can be any size that you'd like but a good rule of thumb is that it should be no smaller than 3' x 3' x 3.'
- A suggestion that was ECHOed to us was that if you eliminate meat and cheese products from the bin, you are far less likely to have the big marauding animals checking out the bin for a possible dinner.
- Then, see if someone can help you find (or buy) a wooden pallet. (You can find one at the local food store, or maybe there's one in your garage...if you can find anything in your garage!)
- Make a large wire mesh lining or nest for your heap.
- Lay the pallet in the middle of the wire mesh. The pallet allows air to circulate beneath the heap, which, again, helps the decomposition process.
- Sprinkle a layer (you only need a few inches) of dry leaves, grass clippings or soil on top of the pallet.
- Every few days, dump your food compost bucket onto the middle of the pallet.
- To keep those animals away, make a wire mesh cover or bonnet to put over the heap and then cover that with leaves or rocks or whatever you think it'll need to keep beasts away. My son, Rhett, covers the wire mesh of his compost heap with leaves and straw and that seems to do the trick.
- Water your compost heap every few days. You don't have to give it a bath, just keep it moist. When you get to the bathroom section of this book, you'll learn what might be a great source of water.
- Once a week, get a shovel and mix up the mush.
- If you want to build a more elaborate compost bin, check the Internet and look for instructions. One good site might be: http://monsterguide.net/how-to-build-a-compost-bin

How do you know when your compost heap can be used?
Simple: When all of your neighbors have moved away or when you can no longer tell what's what in the heap.

What do you do with it?
Use the compost for something special, like fertilizer, that you add to the soil of indoor or outdoor plants, trees, flowers or vegetable gardens.

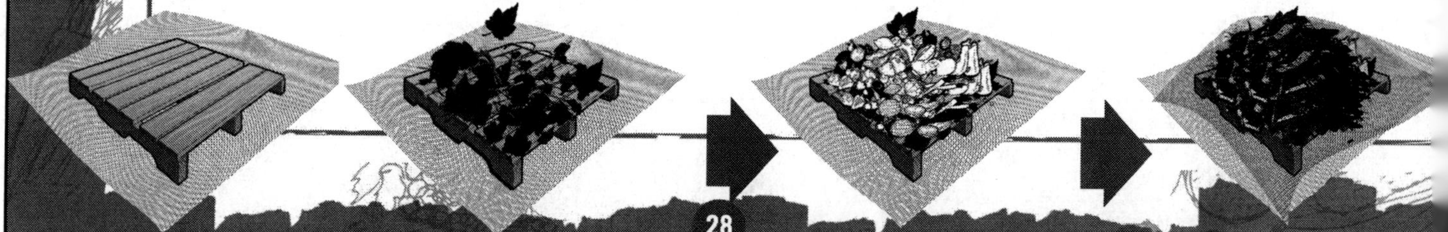

ECO-ACTION Experiments

Now that you are **"Compo-Stars,"** you can conduct some cool experiments at home or **ECHO** to your school.

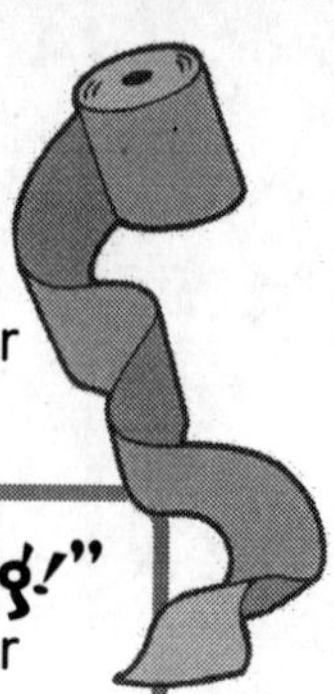

Experiment No. 1: "You're A Good Egg!"
Bury an uncooked egg in the middle of your compost heap. Since it's located in a warm, sunny place, it can really heat up fast. It's not unusual for a heap to reach between 125°F and 140°F. Leave the egg alone for one week (don't dig it up to check on it), and be careful not to break it when turning your compost over with a shovel! In just one week —*voilà!* Your compost heap has probably hard-boiled your egg. In fact, it could only take a few days, but give it the extra time just to make sure that it's done. Please don't eat the egg. Believe me... you do NOT want to experience food poisoning.

Here's something else to try. This experiment will demonstrate how long it takes for certain things to decompose.

Experiment No. 2:
"How Long before It's Gone?"

- Find a part of your yard or ask your science teacher to find a part of the schoolyard for this **ECO-EFFECT experiment.**

  Disclaimer: *Don't disturb roots or rootlets. Also, use a spot that's already cleared, like a lawn.*

- Get a small journal in which to record your findings of how long it takes for things to decompose.
- Some items you can bury are (or come up with your own list):
  - Orange
  - Carrot
  - Egg
  - Tea bag
  - Cigarette butt
  - Wool glove or sock
  - Roll of toilet paper
  - Sneaker
  - Foam cup
  - Disposable baby diaper
  - Tin can
  - Plastic water bottle
  - Plastic grocery bag
  - Aluminum can

Small Disclaimer: *We know that most of these items will pollute the earth, but sometimes you* have to do experiments to prove the point.

- Collect some plastic bottles or jars and cut out small rectangular pieces to make signs. Tape those to Popsicle sticks and, using a permanent marker, label each one with the items you choose, so you know where you have buried them.
- Make a hole for each item, about 1 foot beneath the earth.
- Bury each item.
- Cover each item with dirt.
- Place your Popsicle sign in the ground on top of each item.
- Visit the site once a month and carefully dig up each item. Note its decaying progress in your journal and then rebury each item. Make sure to replace the sign if you took it off before digging.
- If you are at school, you will pass your journal on to the next year's science class, so leave it with your teacher at the end of the school year.
- Here are some hints about how long it takes for some things to decay/biodegrade:
  - The tea bag should be gone in a few months.
  - The orange should decay in six months.
  - The cigarette butt will probably take 10 years.
  - The tin can will take about 100 years.
  - The aluminum can might take up to 500 years.
  - The plastic grocery bag could take 1,000 years to decay.
  - The foam cup will ***NEVER*** decay!

Bathrooms

Don't go with the flow

Let's move on to another very frequently used room, the bathroom. Refer to your EEK list and let's compare notes.

The Big EEK: Wasted Water

- Only 3 percent of the earth's water is fresh. The remaining 97 percent is saltwater and, if not treated, undrinkable.
- Forty percent of the drinkable water supplied to homes is flushed down the toilet.
- If, for a month, one leaky faucet were left to drip in only 3 percent of U.S. households, 95 million gallons of fresh water would go down the drain—enough to provide a year's supply of drinking water to 400,000 people.
- If you take 10-minute showers, you could be wasting enough water—over the course of a year—to fill a backyard pool.
- If one old toilet in every home in the United States were replaced with a new High Efficiency Toilet (HET), we'd save more than 900 billion gallons of water per year—equal to more than two weeks of flow over Niagara Falls.
- If you have an old toilet (and just how do you figure that out? If you didn't see a new one installed, consider that yours is old), it uses approximately 6 gallons of water every time it's flushed, which means a lot of water is wasted here. There is a way to waste less water, though. First, find a plastic, screw-top bottle. (It should be about half-gallon in size.) Then, clean it out and take off all the labels. Next, fill the bottle about halfway with sand or small stones. (No, your brother's little treasures are not a good idea and neither is your sister's hidden stash of lipstick.) Finally, put the container in a corner of the toilet tank, making sure that your invention does not interfere with any of the toilet's parts. Once you've got it in the right place, your new gadget will take up room in the tank, so it will fill up with less water. As a result, less wasted water goes down the toilet with every flush. Pretty neat idea, huh?

Earn EEPs: Here Are Some Tips For Your Taps

To avoid those wasted water **EEKS**, get to work.

- Never leave the tap running while you brush your teeth.
- Don't use the toilet as a garbage can. In other words, if you toss in a tissue or cotton ball, DON'T FLUSH until someone actually *uses* the toilet.
- Take shorter showers and don't leave the water running. Instead:
    - Wet yourself and then turn off the water
    - Soap your body and shampoo your hair
    - Turn the water back on and rinse
- Get a bucket and put it in the shower or tub. While you're waiting for the water to heat up, let the running water fill the bucket. Right before the temperature is warm enough for you, turn the water off, take the bucket out and leave it next to the shower or tub. When you're done, dried and dressed, take the bucket out of the bathroom and give the plants (indoor or outdoor) or your compost heap a drink. **Hint:** If you spill the water all over the living room, you might not get an opportunity to do this again...so walk slowly ...very, very slowly.

Laundry Rules Make Every Drop Count

Just in case you never actually did the laundry or thought that it was done by gnomes in the middle of the night, get out your GPS system and figure out where the dirty clothes are cleaned in your house.

The Big, Expensive EEK:
Wasting Water and Energy

Remember all that talk about throwing things "out" and that "out" was a nice way of saying "landfills"? Guess what happens when you decide to clean clothes? Well, unless you take your stuff to a stream and beat it with a rock, you're going to take your stinky clothes, toss them in a washing machine (at home or in a Laundromat), add chemicals that will make things appear brighter and whiter, turn the machine on to "hot" and let 'er rip. Just to make your whites whiter and your colors brighter, you're sending chemicals into the water supply. (We're talking pollution!)

- Ninety percent of a washing machine's energy is spent heating water. That means the less wash that your family does, especially using hot water, the less water and energy will be used.
- Using a dryer adds a lot to your family's electricity bill. It gets even worse if you either over- or under-load the machine. Most of us just set that timer switch to automatic and let the dryer run until "the cows come home."
- Using your clothes dryer's timer to stop drying cycles can potentially create unnecessary wear to clothes and increase energy costs as a result of over-drying.
- Letting the lint collect until you have enough puffy stuff to make a sweater for a pet isn't good. Why? Lint in the screen makes it harder for the warm air to do its job.
- Top-loading washers and dryers use a lot of water and electricity. They cannot handle very large loads. According to the U.S. Environmental Agency (EPA), front-loading washing machines use 40 percent less water and up to 50 percent less energy than top-loading ones.

Did You Know?

The gas that powers things like dryers is different from the gas that powers things like cars. ***Natural gas*** powers dryers. ***Gasoline*** powers cars.

What If I Send It Away EEK:
Dry Cleaning?

Think you can avoid the energy and water waste by sending everything out to the cleaners? WRONG. Dry cleaning uses tons of energy and environmentally un-cool chemicals. But if you do have to use them, just say "No!" to those plastic bags. Bring a reusable garment bag.

Did You Know?

300,000,000 single use plastic bags from the dry cleaners go into U.S. landfills every year?

Earn EEPs:

- If you wash two loads of laundry a week and switch from hot to cold water, you can save more than 3,300 gallons of hot water a year (and I guarantee that will show up on the utility bills that you've been tracking).
- Don't over-dry your clothes—dry is dry.
- Go one better. Give the dryer a vacation and let your clothes air dry. You can save 50 to 75 cents a load!
- Use a clothes dryer with a moisture sensor instead of a timer, so that the dryer will stop running as soon as the clothes are dry.
- If you go with the dryer, make sure that the lint screen is cleaned after every use. Keeping the airflow high makes things dry faster. Be an **ECO-ACTION** Hero and let everyone know that with a clean filter, your family can save 5 percent on their electricity bill.
- If possible, have your parents look into buying front-loading washers and dryers. Over the course of five years, an estimated $550 would be saved as a result of using less water, energy and detergent. However, if your family can not afford the initial cost of new energy-efficient machines, you may have to take a slightly less dramatic action, but trust me—they will still save some money and earn **EEPs**. You can **ECHO** to everyone in the family and make a sign for the laundry room (or wherever your washer and dryer are stashed) that reads:

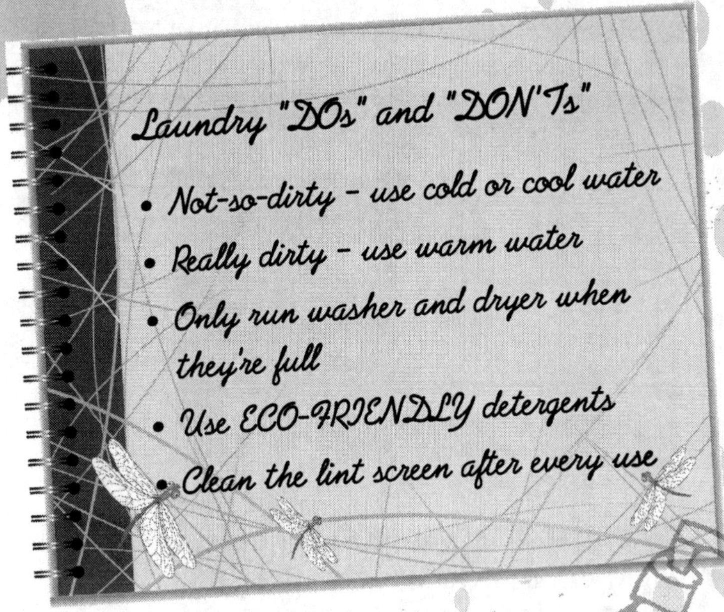

- Score an **EEP** by searching for a "green" dry cleaner that uses less harmful chemicals. (They do exist, but your parents can **ECHO** to you to explain that "green" may not really be "green.")

More Sticky Business

OK, this could go anywhere in the book, but since chewed gum usually ends up on the ground or stuck to your clothes (yes, I know it's not *yours*), we'll discuss this sticky business now.

In order for gum to *not* end up on the ground or stuck to your clothes/shoes, be sure to throw it in the *regular* trash can, *not* in your compost bucket. (Gum belongs on the list that's labeled "DON'Ts.")

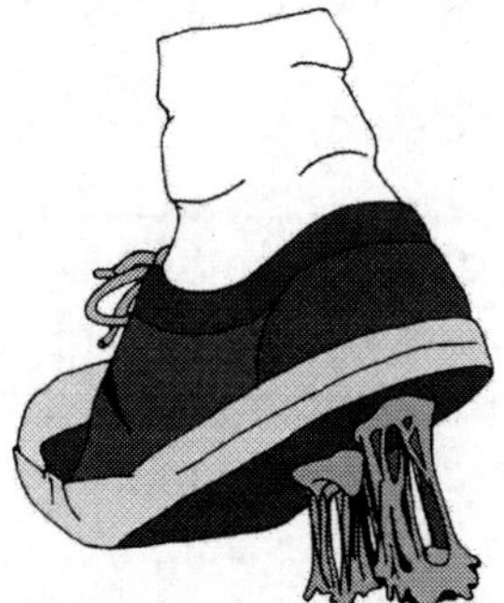

Did You Know?

The average person in the United States chews 190 sticks of gum a year. If you multiply that by every person in the United States, you would come up with 57 billion sticks of gum. Do you have any idea how massive the mess would be if it all ended up on the ground? Try imagining a patch 4 miles wide and 6 miles long.

Throughout the House Electricity and Heating/Cooling

I bet that when you and your parents went through the house looking for EEKs, you found lots of wasted electricity and even more wasted energy flying out the window (literally).

High Voltage EEKs: Electricity

- Name any appliance or gadget in your house that uses electricity, and I'll bet as an **ECO-ACTION** Detective, you'll discover that it wastes more electricity than you'd ever imagine possible.
- A color TV left on standby can eat up 85 percent of the energy it uses when it is actually turned on. Similarly, a DVD player left on standby uses almost the same amount of electricity as it does when playing your favorite movie (or even a movie you don't like).
- Lighting accounts for between 5 and 10 percent of the total energy use in an average house in the U.S.
- In one day, your refrigerator uses as much energy as a washer and dryer, dishwasher and CD player put together!

- Every time you open your fridge door—or indeed your freezer's door—it allows cold air to escape. If this is allowed to happen for more than a few moments the thermostat inside the fridge or freezer, sensing that too much cold air has gone, will turn on the fridge's motor and compressor pump to cool down the new air. The more the compressor pump and its motor are forced to run unnecessarily, the more electricity is used. By playing hide-and-seek in the refrigerator, you are wasting both energy and money.

DID YOU KNOW?

The average family in the U.S. opens their fridge about 8,000 times per year.

- Okay, you don't plug some stuff in but it does require energy to make it work. I'm not talking hamsters running on wheels to create foot-powered electricity. So, what am I talking about? Well, one of the most common things that people use when there are "no plugs required," are batteries. Disposable batteries contain toxins that can seep into landfills and pollute our land and water supply.

Earn EEPs:

- When it comes to buying electronic stuff, look for the ENERGY STAR logo or compare energy efficiency at www.energystar.gov.
- Consider buying electronics that can be recycled in order to avoid adding additional toxins to the earth. Go to www.epeat.net to find an **ECO-FRIENDLY** "report card" on a *gazillion* products. Some computer, printer and cell phone manufacturers have even set up their own recycling programs, so try to buy their products when it makes **ECOnomic** sense.

Eco-Action Activity:

Go room to room, filling in the blanks on your list with all the gadgets that can be turned off when they're not in use. Here are a few items to get you started:

- TV
- Computer
- Video gaming system
- CD player
- ____________________
- ____________________
- ____________________

- Now, go into the kitchen and unplug all those little appliances (like coffee makers and toasters). They are using energy just to keep that little red light lit. (If you ever want to be fed another meal in your house...DO NOT unplug the refrigerator or freezer! The same goes for the oven and dishwasher. Walk away. Do not attempt to even find their outlets. Trust me on this advice...I'm a mother.

- The last one out of the room has to turn off the lights.
- At one of your Family Meetings, consider buying and installing timers for the lights, replacing light switches with motion sensors or even just installing some solid-state dimmer switches. All of these **ECO-investments** will pay off!.
- Turn off the lights near windows and "Let the Sun Shine In." (Ask your parents about that song. I apologize because they will probably sing a few bars and make you cringe.)
- Dust off light bulbs. (NOTE TO SELF: If you don't want a burned or bloody hand make sure to wait until the bulbs are cool. Hot ones burn and break easily. *OUCH!*)
- Replace five of your most regularly-used light bulbs with compact fluorescent lamps (CFLs), it will prevent the creation of greenhouse gases. If every household in the U.S. did this, it would save enough energy to provide light to more than 15 million homes for a whole year!

- Switch from disposable batteries to rechargeable ones. Your parents will probably have to buy the battery charger. Before the next Family Meeting do some research online to find out how much one of these gizmos cost.

DID YOU KNOW?

One rechargeable battery lasts as long as 25 regular batteries. Most rechargeable batteries can be charged 100 times before you need to replace them.

How Cool are You?:

Temperature Control EEKs

- Half of your home's energy bills are due to heating and cooling. In fact, 10 percent of the bill is probably caused by air leaking through the ceilings, floors, walls and windows.
- Each degree over 68°F can increase the amount of energy you use to heat your home by 3 percent. That means that if it costs your family $500 a month to heat your house in the winter, a 3 percent savings is $15 a month and $180 a year...no small change! So, check the thermostat's temperature setting.

- When it's hot do you let your air conditioners run at full blast? Do you think that room fans are so "yesterday"? Consider this; you can save 80 to 90 percent on cooling costs if you turn off the AC. If every home in San Diego with air conditioning used fans for just three hours on one warm summer day, the energy saved could power over 3,000 homes for one full month!

Earn EEPs:

- Some of the major air leaks can be fixed with weather stripping tape or caulk. At one of your Family Meetings, you might even decide to use some of the **EEP** savings for new doors or windows.

REBATE

DID YOU KNOW?

The government is giving out rebates for some energy-saving replacement windows and doors? It's **ECO**nomically smart to be **ECO**logically smart!

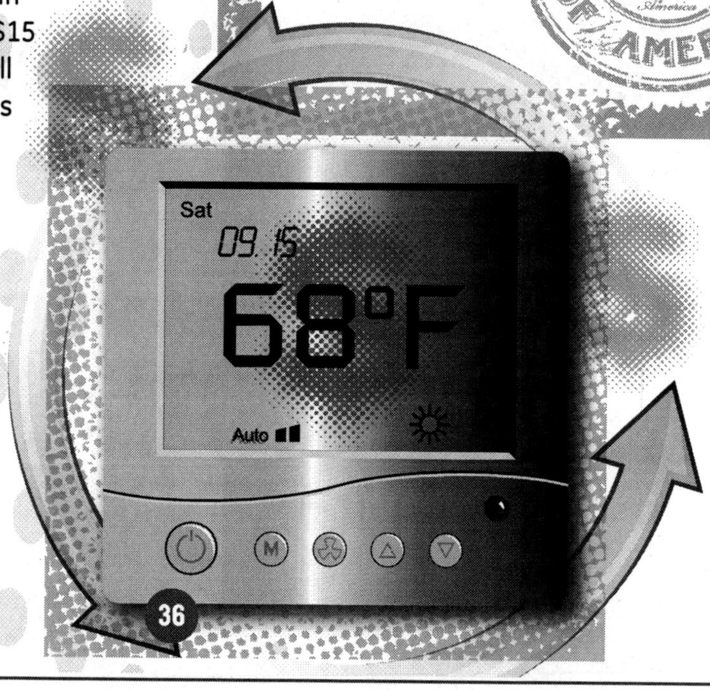

- One of the easiest ways to make your house more energy efficient and save on those heating and cooling bills is to make sure that the house has good insulation. Remember when you began your work as an **ECO-ACTION** Detective, you checked out the first floor of your home for leaks? If you found any, get to work, earn a few **EEPs**, and find out what you can do. Start by researching insulation (remember R-values?) **HERE'S A Tip:** go to www.energysavers.gov to see what's recommended.

- If a thermostat is near an open window, it will give a *false* hot or cold reading. For a correct reading, make sure that the window is completely closed.

- At a Family Meeting discuss investing in a programmable thermostat that will adjust the temperature to energy-saving settings throughout the day and night.

- Don't block heating vents. To get the most heat out of your radiators, make sure that they're dusted or vacuumed regularly. Also, don't put your stuff on top of them...radiators are not shelves.

- In the winter, lower your thermostat's temperature setting by 3° during the day and 5° at night. In the summer, raise the thermostat's temperature setting by the same number of degrees. If your family is OK with this, and no one has either frozen or melted, you're going to become an **ECO-ACTION** Hero when the energy bills arrive.

- Pay attention to the air conditioners. Keep those vents clean and clear, move furniture away from the vents. Set it and leave it. By selecting 78°F instead of 72°F, you can save up to 12 percent on your cooling costs.

- Use Mother Nature. Get a compass or a portable GPS (some cell phones have a built-in navigation system you can use) and go around the house or apartment to figure out which windows face north, east, west and south. On the windows facing east, keep the shades open in the winter (to let in the light) and drawn in the summer (to shade your room and keep out unwanted heat during the day). If you don't have a compass or a GPS, get up at sunrise to see which side of the house gets the sun first. That's east! To test your hypothesis, check out which window gets the sunset each night—that's west!

DID YOU KNOW?

There are new gizmos that can help you and your family cut energy bills. Want to find out which appliances use the most electricity? Go to the website Kill-A-What (www.p3international.com). The Kill-A-Watt only costs $20. Want to check out the entire house? Black & Decker has a $100 Power Monitor that will show you how much electricity is being used in your whole house...or you can check out The Energy Detective (www.theenergydetective.com) that costs $120 that also displays your energy consumption in kWh.

Gardening A Gift to the World

Gardening is more than just "smelling the roses." Next time you walk out the door, look around. That patch of green can be made even "greener" ...and you can save some "green" along the way.

Ugly EEKs:

- By not composting the 24 million tons of leaves and grass clippings that we just throw out each year, we are adding to the already over-flowing landfills.
- If one of your chores is to mow the lawn, and you use a gas or electric lawn mower, you're consuming fossil fuels and emitting greenhouse gases. If you must use a power model, make sure it is a mulching mower that reduces grass clippings.
- By using heavy-duty chemical fertilizers, we are polluting crops with residue and potentially poisoning our food. These non-environmentally friendly fertilizers also seep into the ground and pollute the water, as well.

Did You Know?

According to the EPA, the average gas-powered lawn mower emits just as much pollution into our environment as 43 cars being driven 12,000 miles each.

- A garden hose or sprinkler can use almost as much water in an hour as an average family of four uses in one day.

Earn EEPs:

- Push it! Leave the power mower in the garage and see if you or one of your neighbors has one of those old push mowers. Besides being better for the environment, it'll sure help you build muscles.

- Ask your parents to consider swapping a natural lawn for a fake one. It may not sound so **ECO-Friendly** but consider this: no mowing, no fertilizing and best of all, in many parts of the country, no water is used! Find out more at www.ecowaterlessgrass.com.
- If you must fertilize, use organic fertilizers (and your compost muck) properly. It's best to apply fertilizer when the soil is moist. After you spread the fertilizer on your plants or lawn, you'll need to water it lightly. This will help the fertilizer move into the root zone where it can be available to the plants, instead of possibly being blown or washed away were it to stay on top of

the soil. Watch the weather and avoid applying the fertilizer immediately before heavy rain is predicted to arrive. Too much rain (or sprinkler water) will take the nutrients away from the lawn's root zone. Use the least amount of fertilizer necessary and apply it in small, frequent applications. An application of 2 pounds of fertilizer five times per year is better than 5 pounds of fertilizer twice a year.

- Ask your parents to leave the grass clippings on the lawn after it is mowed. Not only are the clippings healthy for your lawn, but they can also reduce the amount of fertilizer that is needed. For example, a 4,000-square-foot lawn that is fertilized with grass clippings would need 25 percent less chemical fertilizers for the same effect.

Eco-Action Activity:

Make your own ECO-FRIENDLY lawn fertilizer. Some of these ingredients sound crazy, but they're proven to work.

Recipe for Making Your Own Fertilizer

1 cup of (regular, not light) beer (Ask your parents to get it for you and NO tasting allowed!)

1 cup of ammonia or fabric softener

1 cup of baby shampoo

1 cup of organic liquid lawn food

1/2 cup of molasses or corn syrup

(In case you're wondering, ammonia provides nitrates, soap improves spread, and beer encourages microbial activity.)

Mix, spray onto your lawn and enjoy the natural greenery.

- Since birds are natural bug eaters, instead of using pesticides on your lawn and garden, ask your parents if you can put up a birdhouse. For extra points, try making your own.
- Buy some ladybugs. They are fantastic, natural pest-killers for your garden. How can you get them? Look online.
- Instead of letting rainwater go to waste in places like your driveway, catch it in a barrel. When the yard or garden starts getting dry, use this "gift from the skies" along with the water that you've been collecting from the shower.
- Before your parents buy outdoor flowers and shrubs, do a bit of research to find out which plants need the least amount of water to live. How do you find out? You can either go online or ask at the garden center. If one in every 100 households chose drought-tolerant species of plants almost 600 million gallons of water could be saved—enough to provide water to all of New York City's residents for a whole day.
- Make an organic herb and vegetable garden. All you have to do is mix regular soil with some of your compost and then plant your "salad-to-be." You can create your garden in your backyard or in containers on your apartment's deck, if it gets a lot of sun.
- **ECHO** to your parents to help them save more than 20 percent on their air-conditioning bill each year by helping them plant two shade trees. Plant one tree on the west side of your house and the other on the east side. (Remember which side is which?) The trees will have to reach 25 feet tall before they provide enough shade, but they'll *never* grow if you don't plant them...so get started!
- Plant a tree. For your next birthday, ask your parents to buy you a sapling to plant in your yard. Do some research to make sure it will be a tree that grows well in your area.

Did You Know?

There are more than 1 million city-community gardens in the U.S., according to Mrs Obama.

Create a Family Tradition

Plant trees! When I was your age, my parents let me plant a crab apple tree in our backyard. It had beautiful pink flowers in the spring, and we made crab apple jelly in the fall. Now that I am a parent, my kids buy me a tree for Mother's Day every year. It's a great gift!

Consider this, instead of buying or cutting down a tree at Christmas, we gave Grandma Mary a small, potted evergreen every year. There are now almost 20 huge, healthy trees growing on her property!

Eco-Action Activity:
Green Roofs

How do these special roofs shield buildings from heat and cold, while also reducing energy usage? Try Googling "Green Roofs." What country started the movement? Do you know where the biggest one is? (It's listed in the Guinness World Records.) See if you can do an extra credit report for school or just ECHO to your family, friends and teachers about this cutting-edge technology.

The ECO-Chain—One Link at a Time

Remember **ECO-EDEN,** where everything was in balance? If left undisturbed, the **ECO-System** creates a chain, and each link in the chain is essential for the whole system to work. One small link in the **ECO-Chain** is right in *your own* environment—on your lawn or in the park—and you may not have ever thought about them. Earthworms!

One goal of this book is to help you **ECHO** to the world, so that you'll help to change it in positive ways. Yet another goal is for you to become aware of your environment in new ways. That new awareness will help you appreciate how important and beautiful each link is to the whole.

OK, go out to your lawn (if you have one) or find some grass in the park. When you get to a place that looks clean (no bird droppings or dog poop), lie down and take a *really* close look at what's around you. Did you know there were so many shades of green in the grass? How about the rocks? Notice the different shapes, textures and clarity. If you're super lucky, you might even see an insect wing or an animal hair.

Now, go take a small shovel and dig a very, VERY small hole. (Hint: I suggest that you find a spot that's *not* in the middle of your front lawn. Most parents aren't thrilled with *animals* digging up their lawns. They'll probably have a fit if *you* do it!) What you're looking for is an earthworm. If it's just rained, you'll really be in luck—but it may not be a lucky day for the worm. Why? Well, after a hard rain, the water soaks into the ground and floods the earthworm's burrow, forcing it to leave home so it doesn't drown. If it's a light rain, the worm actually sucks in the soil and then spews it out on top of its burrow—making tiny mud piles. If you look closely, you'll see it.

Who Knew?
Earthworm—Boy or Girl?

Earthworms can grow to 11 inches in length? Look carefully, and you'll see lines or "segments" along their body. If you count the segments and the 15th segment is open, it's a boy. If the opening is on the 14th segment, it's a girl.

Rita's Butterfly Garden:

Have you ever watched a butterfly flit from flower to flower sipping nectar through its long curled proboscis? It doesn't seem to have a care in the world other than where to find the next nectar source. Did you ever stop to think why that butterfly exists? Is it purely for decorative purposes or does it have a job? Have you by any chance noticed that as we have more and more houses we have fewer and fewer butterflies? Did you know that butterflies, just like bees, are pollinators? They help to transfer pollen from flower to flower so that we have more flowers and fruits.

Do you like to see butterflies in your garden? How do you get them to come to your garden? Many people know that if you plant a butterfly bush you will likely have butterflies visit. Plants with nectar serve as butterfly gas stations. But, did you know that is exactly what they will do – just visit. If you want butterflies to live in your yard, you must plant host plants. Host plants are unique to each type of butterfly. They are the plant that the caterpillar eats. Host plants are necessary for the butterfly metamorphosis. A mother butterfly knows that her babies are very picky eaters. They will only eat one to two types of plants. For example, the Eastern Black Swallowtail will happily sip nectar from a variety of sources including Butterfly Bush or Butterfly Weed Flowers, BUT if you plant a Bronze Fennel plant the female will lay her eggs on it. You can then watch the very hungry caterpillars eat and eat and eat until they turn into a chrysalis. About 10 days later you can watch the butterfly emerge with its large abdomen and very small wings. It will hang on a branch or wall fluttering its wings until the fluids transfer into them and the sun hardens them. The butterfly is then ready to flit from flower to flower. It will unfurl its long curled proboscis in order to suck the nectar from the far reaches of the neck of the flower.

BECOME A BUTTERFLY HOST

If you and your parents plant host plants, you will have butterflies as permanent residents of your garden. It is remarkably easy. Just plant a nectar plant and a host plant. You can even do this in a pot if you don't have a garden spot. My list will give you tips on getting started.

More importantly, we are destroying more and more host plants each year. Fields are turned into housing or commercial developments. Governments spray roadsides for broad leaved plants to make them look nicer but in doing so they destroy many native plants that would host butterfly populations. Butterflies are even killed each year by cars. For these reasons, it is becoming increasingly important for people to plant both host and nectar plants in their yards to help sustain our butterfly populations. These native plants add beauty and diversity to your yard. They will also attract birds and other beneficial visitors to your yard.

Adopt a Butterfly - A really remarkable experience for your children and you is to adopt a butterfly. And, if you plant host plants in your yard, it will cost you next to nothing for this natural entertainment year after year after year. Plant a butterfly bush and a bronze fennel plant. Then just wait and watch for caterpillars to eat the airy bronze fronds of the plant. Or, if you are lucky, you will get to see the mother butterfly curling her abdomen under her body as she deposits the eggs on the plant. This is great fun! If you see a butterfly near a host plant, start watching, but no touching! If they are there, they are getting ready to lay their eggs. Once the caterpillar emerges from the egg, it eats the shell first for protein and then starts to gnaw on the host plant. It will eat and eat and eat. What fun! Then it gets tired because its clothes fit too tightly. As it rests, it sheds its skin (known as molting) to find a new one beneath the old. Now that the skin is loose, that caterpillar can start eating again. It actually does this five times. These growth spurts or cycles are known as instars. After all of that eating, shedding and growing the caterpillar is ready for a nap. It crawls to a high spot and attaches to a wall or stick. Then the miraculous transformation of becoming a chrysalis occurs. This is simply awesome to watch! Adults, children and even teenagers are simply amazed to watch this occurrence. Many people spend most of their lives without witnessing the chrysalis formation or the emergence of the butterfly. ECHO this to everyone! After approximately 10 days, the chrysalis will split open and a butterfly will emerge.

Tips for getting started:

- **Find a sunny spot to plant a nectar plant.** Most people begin with a butterfly bush. You can use a container plant.
- **Now choose a host plant.** The easiest is parsley or bronze fennel. These host the Eastern Black Swallowtail butterfly. I recommend this one for starters because if you run out of host plant, you can buy parsley in the store. But be sure to wash it, as my family and I have lost a whole bunch of caterpillars to store bought parsley — which means it had something poisonous on it.
- **DO NOT use pesticides or other harmful chemicals in your garden.** Both the caterpillar and butterfly are extremely sensitive and easily killed.
- **Keep a close eye on the plants so you can enjoy your visitors.** I recommend taking your caterpillars indoors and feed them in a container with a breathable lid. Caterpillars have few ways to defend themselves so we like to help them out. Wasps, spiders and birds are among the many predators.

Plant List for Beginners:

- **Butterfly bush** *(Buddleia davidii)* – nectar plant.
- **Bronze fennel** *(Foeniculum vulgare)* – host plant. for Eastern Black Swallowtail.
- **Butterfly weed** *(Asclepias spp.)* – nectar plant and host for monarchs.
- **Coneflower** *(Echinacea spp.)* – long blooming nectar plant and host for silvery checkerspot.
- **Tall verbena** *(Verbena bonariensis)* – great nectar plant.
- **Milkweed** *(Asclepias spp.)* – necessary host for Monarch survival and also great for nectar.
- **Pipevine** *(Aristolochia macrophylla)* – host to Pipevine Swallowtail which is the coolest caterpillar alive.
- **Spicebush** *(Lindera benzoin)* – host to Spicebush Swallowtail which is also a really cool caterpillar.
- **Sweet bay magnolia** *(Magnolia virginiana)* – host to Tiger Swallowtail.
- **Willows** *(Saliz spp.)* – host for Red-Spotted Purple and Viceroy.

Rita bought me this wonderful book for learning butterfly and butterfly gardening basics: *The Life Cycle of Butterflies: From Egg to Maturity, a Visual Guide to 23 Common Garden Butterflies* by Judy Burris and Wayne Richards. My son, Rhett, and I are reading, learning, and ECHOing together.

ECHO to Your School
Teach a Teacher

Schools are a great place to ECHO. Here are examples of how some schools across the country are becoming more ECO-EFFECTIVE:

*North Side Elementary School—
Fort Lauderdale, Florida*
To save energy, this school has lights that automatically adjust to natural light and a "white roof" to reflect the sun and heat, reducing the need for air conditioning.

*Harold Oliver Primary School—
Portland, Oregon*
Every year, students are taught proper recycling procedures for the cafeteria and classroom. They are also learning about **ECOlogy** in their school lessons. Second graders oversee the recycling process in the cafeteria, and one class even manages the composting of fruit and vegetable waste.

*Indian Prairie School District 204—
Chicago, Illinois*
Their "Energy Management Program" works as a result of students, faculty and staff **ECHOing** their behavior to each other and to others. Through their projects that have incorporated such things as solar power, waterless urinals and "daylighting" (using natural light in place of electric lighting), this school district has helped to avoid $1.5 million in energy costs!

*Far Hills Country Day School—
Far Hills, New Jersey*
This school is attempting to become a "net zero" energy user within the next 10 years. Students are encouraged to **ECHO** their ideas and, as a result, the "Upper School Energy Task Force" was formed. This group of 6th, 7th and 8th graders survey each room in the school to calculate per-room energy use, are making a list of high-consumption areas and are planning a ticketing program to motivate people to do their part. (They are serious about their **EEKs** and **EEPs!**)

*The Martin Luther King, Jr. Middle School—
Berkeley, California*
They created an *Edible Schoolyard* to replace the pre-packaged, microwaveable meals that were being served from a shack in the parking lot. They now have a one-acre organic garden and a kitchen-classroom. In the garden, students are involved in all aspects of planting and cultivation and in the kitchen-classroom, they prepare, serve and eat food, some of which they have grown themselves.

Consider how much fun creating an Edible Schoolyard might be. ECHO the idea and see what happens. It sure beats sitting at a desk and reading from a textbook, doesn't it?

Eco-Action Activity:

"Dis" the Fast Food. Bring on the Slow Food Movement.

Slow Food is an idea, a way of living and a way of eating. It is a global, grassroots movement with thousands of members around the world that links the pleasure of food with a commitment to community and the environment.

To learn more about Slow Food in Schools, visit www.slowfoodusa.org

ECHO these ideas at school and with your classmates:

- Ride your bike, take a bus or carpool. If you and everyone else gets involved, thousands of gallons of gasoline will be saved on a daily basis. (If you and your friends ride your bikes, you'll all be getting great exercise, too!)

- Don't clean erasers in the classroom. Why? Ever breathe in chalk dust? Yuck! Aside from being unhealthy (especially for kids who have asthma or other respiratory illnesses that make it hard for them to breathe) chalk dust also makes the rooms harder to clean. There's even a good **ECOnomic** reason... if the dust gets into computer equipment, it could cause some mighty expensive damage. **ECHO** this idea for an **ECOlogical** *and* **ECOnomic EEP!**

- Avoid using crayons made from paraffin wax (they're petroleum-based), and, if you must use markers, use those that have nontoxic ink with refillable heads.

- Use only pencils that are made from recycled material and sold either loose or in recyclable packaging. Also, use only refillable pens. Every year, people in the United States throw out 1.6 billion pens. If these 1.6 billion pens were placed end-to-end, the distance would stretch more than 150,000 miles—the equivalent of crossing the Pacific Ocean (from Los Angeles to Tokyo) more than 25 times!

- When it comes to buying school supplies—adhesive notes, binders, file folders, notebooks, paper, plastic rulers, scissors, tape dispensers, wastebaskets, paper clips—make sure that they're made from recycled materials.

- Avoid buying polyvinyl chloride (PVC), which is commonly called "vinyl." This type of plastic is found in some backpacks, folder covers and raincoats. Be a smart shopper because many experts think that this plastic may contain toxins that can be harmful to your immune system. These things can be difficult to recycle, too.

- Ask your teachers to keep the classroom temperatures at 69°F in the winter and 73°F in the summer. If every room in your school and every school in the district, and every school the state and the country, did this one simple thing, think of the **ECO-EFFECT.** Both energy and money will be saved.

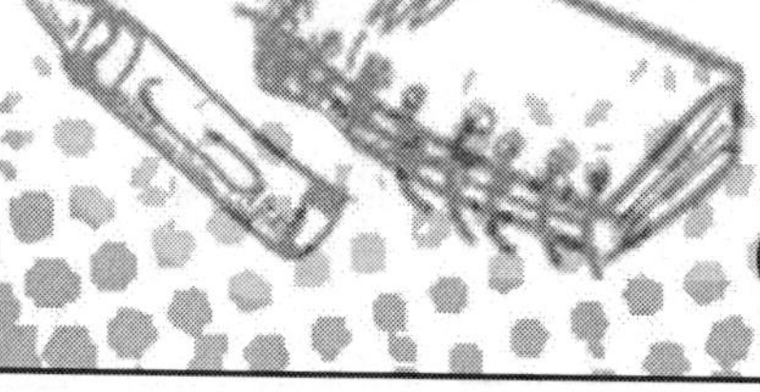

- Instead of throwing away food that you're not going to eat, find a food donation program. If each of the 3,600 charter schools in the U.S. participated in one of these programs, the total savings could feed one meal a day—for an entire year—to more than 2 million starving people. Can you imagine how many people could be fed if all schools participated in one of these programs?
- As you learned earlier, bring your lunch to school in reusable containers.
- Recycle and encourage everyone else (including teachers) to participate.
- Make sure the lights are turned off when a room (or building) is empty, and **ECHO** to others (teachers, custodians, students, etc.) to do the same.

"Hoof It" to School

You can figure out your ECO-EFFECT by simply walking back and forth to school each day. Here's a simple math problem to figure out how: Let's assume your parents' car gets 20 miles per gallon and that gasoline costs $4.00 per gallon. How much will you save in both gasoline usage and money if you walked both ways?

Example: You live 1 mile from school x 2 (back and forth) X both ways (to and from your home and school) x 5 days per week = 20 miles per week.

20 miles per week = 1 gallon of gas or $4.00 a week in savings x 40 weeks of school = $160.00 per year.

Note: *If you go back and forth for sports, class plays, music lessons, etc., start to double, triple or even quadruple these numbers.*

Sustainability: The True "Blue"

You hear the word "Sustainability" a lot. One way to think of "Sustainability" is that it means "to keep things going so that we don't run out of limited resources". In the **ECO-Effect**, I've mostly focused on two parts of sustainability: **ECOnomics** and **ECOlogy**. We call this "Green". But when you focus on the total sustainable picture, people have come up with a new word, "Blue". "Blue" includes all people and their needs to make the world a better sustainable place for all living things. If we focus on how sustainability can happen, the only way it can is to have people all over the world "**ECHO**" together to make things change for a better world for everyone. That constant and steady change — forever — is true sustainability.

But just like we have concentrated on making a safe and better world for plants and animals, through responsible **ECOlogy**, we have to make a safe and better world for all people. That total sustainability is a true "**ECHO**" —True "Blue".

I'm involved with two charities that help less fortunate people create sustainable lives so they can "**ECHO**" in a safe and healthy way. So, since I wrote this book, I get to discuss some of the charities I work with. But, I want you, your family, your school . . . to "**ECHO**" to me on my **ECO-ACTION Network** site at www.eco-effect.net/eco-actionnetwork and spread-the-word about how you are making a difference with your charities.

My first charity is the U.S. National Committee for UNIFEM. UNIFEM is a United Nations agency that concentrates on women in developing countries so they can live safe, free and healthy lives. The U.S. National Committee works in the U.S. to support UNIFEM by educating the public, advocating and fundraising.

Many women and girls in the world are not as lucky as we are in the United States. Can you imagine if day-after-day you had to put-up with a bully in your school and you could not report it to anyone? Now imagine that you didn't have enough food to eat or water to drink.

Now imagine it gets even worse. The bully is hurting you, you are tired, weak and sick from not eating and you're also working hard at a job, but not getting paid enough to feed yourself or your family. Sounds impossible? It's not for millions of women and their daughters who live in the developing countries of the world. It's their life. Here are the facts:

- There are about 1.3 billion people living in poverty around the world – that's about 1 out of 6 people on our planet. 70% of these people are women who are living on less than $1.00 a day!
- Women raise their families and work at jobs at the same time. 66% of the world's work is done by women, but they earn less than 5% of the world's income. That means let's say, you have an after-school job, and everyone else is earning $10.00 an hour and you are only earning 50 cents — You wouldn't think that was fair, would you? No way!

This all doesn't seem okay, does it? No, of course not. The United Nations, through some of its organizations like UNIFEM, is trying to make things better.

If women aren't safe from being hurt by other people, or free of disease, or if they can't earn, enough to feed themselves, then they can't focus on earning a living (**ECOnomics**) and taking care of their environment (**ECOlogy**). UNIFEM helps women and girls around the world live free from violence and poverty.

ECHO to your parents and friends at school to see what organizations and causes you want to donate your time or money to. Did you know that by just reading the **ECO-Effect**, you are helping and **ECHO**ing to the U.S. National Committee for UNIFEM? For every book I donate, I will give some money to the U.S. National Committee for UNIFEM and Heifer International. You, your parents, and friends at school can also "**ECHO**" to people who are not as lucky as you: Visit www.unifem-usnc.org.

The **ECHO** has begun!

The "R's" Rejuvenate, Reduce, Reuse, Recycle, React

How is the **ECOlogical cycle**, like planting a tree, similar to an **ECOnomic cycle**? Well, in an **ECOnomic cycle**, when one person earns money and then spends it, another person receives (earns) that spent money, and the cycle continues. Make sense? In an **ECOlogical** cycle, instead of money, elements in nature are continuously cycled. For example, a tree uses the carbon dioxide (CO_2) that's floating along in the atmosphere. Then the tree uses the CO_2 and gives off oxygen, which we need in order to breathe and live. Then, we exhale CO_2, which the trees need. When the trees die, they decompose and form part of the soil that is needed for new trees to grow. Do you see how this type of cycle works and how both cycles are similar?

R = Rejuvenate Our ECOnomy

Companies use recycled materials to make new products and new jobs. It's said that recycling in the United States is a $236 billion a year industry, which has created 26,000 recycling companies that hire more than 1 million people.

What Does "Rejuvenate Our ECOnomy" Mean?

Well, when people work and earn a salary, they start what is called an **"ECOnomic cycle."** It's just like the **ECOlogical cycle** that starts when people plant trees, for example.

This is how it works: Working people have to pay taxes. These taxes go to the government to pay for things like police and fire services. They also pay for the workers who build and repair things like roads and bridges. (Taxes even pay President Obama's salary!) With the salary these tax-paying workers earn, they can also buy food and clothes, pay rent, give money to charity and even go to the movies.

When money is continuously spent on goods and services, it becomes a cycle that, in effect, feeds and runs our **ECOnomy.**

R = Reduce Garbage

The average person in the United States throws away $6\frac{1}{2}$ pounds of garbage every day. Most of it ends up in landfills. Our garbage creates pollution that seeps into the land, air and/or water supply.

Think of ways that you and your family can reduce the amount of garbage that you produce. Then make a list of your ideas and get to work creating EEPs. Here is a start (and you can finish!):

- Use reusable, washable cloth grocery bags instead of plastic or paper bags
- Use a refillable water bottle
- ______________________________
- ______________________________
- ______________________________

R = REUSE, RECYCLE

Recycling uses less energy than making things out of original raw materials.

Here is a list of what you and your family should recycle (with space for you to fill in more!):

- Aluminum and steel cans
- Glass bottles and jars
- Plastic bottles (soda, detergent, aspirin, vitamin, etc.)
- Newspapers
- Magazines
- Junk mail
- Cardboard and cardboard boxes (including milk cartons)
- Electronic equipment or e-waste (computers, cell phones, MP3 players, etc.)
- ______________________________
- ______________________________
- ______________________________

ECHO TO YOUR PARENTS:

Explain to them that they need to be conscious about recycling their e-waste in their offices, as well. They can go online to check out which companies in their area offer that service and they can ECHO to their bosses to make sure their old computers and office supplies don't end up in landfills.

Steps to Recycle:

- Call your local recycling center to see what is recyclable in your town or city.
- Put four cardboard boxes, plastic bins or heavy bags in an out-of-the-way location in your home.
- Make sure everyone knows where they are—in a closet, near a back door, etc.
- Put labels on each box, bin or bag so everyone knows where to put the different recyclables.

Hint: *Always line them up in the same way, so you don't confuse the family. Here is an example:*

DID YOU KNOW?

- During the time it takes you to read this sentence, 50,000 12-ounce aluminum cans were made. (If you're a slower reader, 60,000 cans were made.)
- Recycling a single Sunday edition run of The New York Times would save 75,000 trees.
- If everyone recycled their newspapers every day, we could save about 250 million trees each year.
- All the people in the United States throw away enough trash every minute to fill an average house.

Eco-Action Activity:

Do the Math

Let's say you had one 15-year-old tree, and you made it into grocery bags. You'd be able to make about 700 of them. A typical supermarket would use all of them in an hour. Assume a grocery store is open 24 hours a day, 365 days a year. How many paper bags would it use in a year? OK, you've got your number. Now, figure out many trees it would take to make those bags?

Answer is upside down on the bottom of this page.

R = REACT!

- Each week between Thanksgiving and New Year's Day, people in the U.S. produce 2 million pounds of *just* gift-wrap garbage. If 40 percent of our households used two less sheets of wrapping paper, the savings could "gift wrap" Manhattan. I wrap my gifts in old newspapers, magazines or reusable baskets. If you *really* want to use gift wrapping paper, though, there is recycled paper you can buy.
- If you use newspaper instead of gift wrap – and let's say you and your family give 25 gifts during the holidays — you might spend almost $25 on wrap alone. Remember, the gift wrap gets torn off, hauled away and ultimately ends up in a landfill. On the other hand, your "newspaper wrap" can end up in your compost heap and recycle to nature.
- Avoid using rubber bands. Most are made of synthetic rubber, which is made from fossil fuels. In turn, when rubber bands are burned at the dump, they cause pollution. In North America, 2,200 metric tons of synthetic rubber is used each year. This could make almost a quarter of a million rubber band balls as big as the World's Largest Ball of Twine, which is in Cawker City, Kansas. (**ECHO** to me if you have seen this ball of twine in Kansas. If you have, you may get a mention in my next book for the family that takes the weirdest vacations...and I do NOT want you planning *my* next trip.)

Bags used: 6,132,000 – Trees used: 8,760

Eco-Action Activity:

Trash or Treasures:

Go through your possessions and decide what you do and don't want. Ask your parents to do the same thing. You'll be surprised at how much you can recycle. You could donate some of your things to homeless shelters, The Salvation Army, Goodwill or other charitable organizations. You could also turn your "recyclables" into cash by selling them on eBay or by conducting a garage sale.

Getting Ready for the Big Garage Sale

A garage or yard sale is a great way to recycle and make some money (not to mention making your parents happy). So, clean out your basement, bedroom or attic. Who knows...you might even find that pallet for your compost heap!

You can sell almost anything at a garage sale: books, clothing, computers, furniture, appliances, bicycles, sports equipment, rugs, tools, dolls and other toys. It is not a great idea to be creative when it comes to other people's things, though. You may find your sister's boots or your dad's old golf clubs, but trust me, if you don't want to create a war, step back and ask first before you try to sell anyone else's possessions.

Don't think of it as a chore. The stuff you sell could make a big difference in helping your family reach your **ECO-ACTION** Goals.

All items should be clean and in good working order. You can also ask your friends if they want to sell their stuff. If they say "yes," make sure to keep a good list of what belongs to each of you. Place colored dot stickers on everything in order to tell what belongs to whom. All items with a red dot, for example, might come from Tamika. As each item is sold, look at the colored sticker to know whose item it was and write down the sale price under that person's name. At the end of the garage sale, just add up the prices on each person's list.

Ask your parents to help you with pricing and to explain about bargaining. You want to *sell* the items, not *give* them away. However, you also don't want to end up with too much leftover junk at the end of the sale. Don't overprice your old doll or toy just because it has sentimental value to you. A garage sale is a success if you can end the event with *nothing but money*.

HERE'S HOW TO PRICE THINGS:

For big items, such as a television, figure out approximately what you would pay today if the set was new. Then, take three-quarters off that price. For example, a *new* food processor could cost about $100, but you would price it $25 at a garage sale.

You can help by looking through magazines, catalogs or online to find current prices. You can also help calculate the "garage sale price" of each item.

Stuff that has less value, such as old clothing and books, should be priced to be a "deal." (They should sell quickly.) A dollar or two is fine, unless it was very expensive when new.

Remember, most people who go to garage sales are looking for bargains. So, if a television is "worth" $10, you may want to price it at $15 so you can leave room for bargaining. Ask your parents about creating a win-win situation.

When picking the day for your garage sale, don't pick a holiday. Also be sure to think of a "rain date"—a substitute day in case the weather is bad. To get the word out about your garage sale, you have to let people know about it. How do you do that? Well, you advertise it. You can be in charge of advertising. Ask your parents if you can make easy-to-read signs and post them at busy corners in the neighborhood. Use brightly-colored recycled poster paper and an **ECO-FRIENDLY** marker.

Also, see if you can take advantage of Web Sites that let you post garage sale notices for free. Your local newspaper may also offer free garage sale ads.

It's important to have the address and time of the sale but not a phone number because you don't want to get a ton of calls. If your family is moving, you can say that in the ad, as well. That way, readers will know you really need to sell *everything* and will be motivated to do so!

It's also a good idea to let the neighbors know that you are planning a garage sale. They might decide to join you or just be away for the day.

Before your garage sale starts, make the items you're selling look as good as possible. Items will sell for higher prices if they're clean and nicely displayed. Hang up any clothes and lay other stuff on tarps and tables so people don't have to dig through piles. Allow plenty of time to tag, price and arrange everything.

A lot of people drive by in their cars to check out a sale and see if it's worth stopping. Make sure you place hot-selling items in visible spots.

If there are electrical items for sale, run an extension cord to an outlet in the garage or house so you won't have people inside your home testing to see if your stuff works.

IT'S ON!

So, what happens when people start showing up? (By the way, be prepared for "early birds" who try to buy the items before the sale officially begins.) Anyway, when people arrive, the real bargaining begins. Bargaining should be fun and friendly for everyone, but what happens if a buyer is tough? For example, you may have originally marked a small table $15 but dropped the price to $10 later. Yet, the buyer says that $8 is his last offer. It's fine. You need to keep in mind that the goal is to sell *everything* at the best price possible. If you insist on $10, you might have a real buyer walking away. Then you will have made *no* money. It's better to sell the item for $8—especially at the end of the sale—than to put it back in the basement.

Some shoppers will collect a pile of items and ask you to come up with a bulk discount (for buying so many things at once). If that happens, 20 percent or one-fifth off is fair.

IT'S OVER

Now that the sale is over, you might want to call a Family Meeting to talk about how you did and what you should do with the money that was earned. I know that you might like to take your share and buy something that you've always wanted, but after all the research and work that you've been doing to become a more **ECO-EFFECTIVE** citizen, maybe you've become a bit more **ECOnomically** savvy, as well. Maybe you will **ECHO** and turn those proceeds (and those from the lower energy bills) into making your house, your school or even your community a better place to live. You might decide to replace a leaky window with a new one, donate a tree to a park or even buy the garbage pails for your school lunchroom so that you can create that compost heap. Whatever you decide to do, I'd love you to **ECHO** to me so I can hear about your **ECO-EFFECT** experiences. E-mail me at www.eco-effect.net, and be sure to tell me what you did and how you **ECHOed** – both **ECOnomically** and **ECOlogically**. You've now become an **ECO-ACTION** Hero! Great job!

CHAPTER 14

Back to the Future
A Better Tomorrow

You can now become ECO-ACTION Citizens-of-the-World and earn ECO-EFFECT POINTs (EEPs).

This is a list of activities that you and your family decide to tackle, based on EEKs, with the goal of earning EEPs. You went room by room with your parents to uncover EEKs, and you've researched the costs to fix them. These jobs or EEPs will be done to help save the planet and, in the process, save money by reducing energy costs—the true ECO-EFFECT.

Make sure everyone gets credit for their work. The reward for accomplishing goals can be whatever you've determined it should be, as long as it is **ECOlogically** important. However, it should be something that you ALL agree on at your Family Meeting and can afford.

Here's what a sample **ECO-ACTION Citizen-of-the-World Chart** might look like:

EEK (PROBLEM)	**EEP** (What should be done to fix it?)	**ESTIMATED COST** (To fix the EEK)	**EEP DONE?**	**WHO DID THE EEP?** (names or initials)
Front Window Leak	Caulk It	$3.50	✓	Gavin
Lights Left On	Turn Off Lights	N/A	✓	Naomi Mom Dad
Toilet Uses Too Much Water	Insert Your Bottle Invention (that you made after reading Chapter 8)	N/A	✓	Elijah
Old Light Bulbs	Install Energy-Saving Bulbs	$2.99 (prices vary depending on bulb size/type)	✓	Family

This chart lists the **EEKs** and what needs to be done to correct the problems, including who will do the correcting. When the problems are fixed, the whole family earns **EEPs** and decides how to celebrate their accomplishments at the next Family Meeting.

Remember, an **EEP** is earned for doing something that makes an **ECOlogical** and **ECOnomic** difference for the world. As mentioned before, it could be as simple as making sure the lights are all turned off when you leave a room, taping up your leaky windows, turning off the water when you're brushing your teeth or donating money to save the rainforest.

If any or all of you don't turn off a light or decide to do half a load of laundry, what happens? Nothing. However, if your goal was—and is—to become **ECO-EFFECTIVE**, you have to take responsibility for your actions. Neither money, nor the earth, will be saved if you waste precious resources.

While you and your family are doing these projects, you will be learning and doing important things. You will, in fact, be **ECHOing** knowledge and action to yourself and the world.

Facing Tomorrow

For gazillions of years, we have just gone about our business with little thought to the future. That was bad. We didn't really do it on purpose—we just didn't know any better. Everything seemed fine where we lived, so we didn't even think about it. We thought that each new technological creation was a great thing.

Your MP3 player sure is better than the old AM transistor radio I had at your age, and it's definitely better than my grandmother's phonograph that played records.

Technology is great, but the problem is that we don't think about how to get rid of the old stuff (that we keep replacing with new things) without causing damage to the earth.

Well, we've run out of excuses. I know and you know (and I bet even your younger brothers and sisters know) that we've messed up the planet. In the process, we've created not only **ECOlogical** problems but we've also created **ECOnomic** problems, as well.

Now is the time for you to make that ripple bigger and your **ECHO** louder. For example, share with your friends what you've done at home or suggest to your science teacher what the class can do. You can also write letters to the leaders of your community, the heads of companies and even your government representatives. Ask them to get involved and be ready to go out there with your suggestions and recommendations.

If your parents have "Take Your Child to Work Days" at their office, go with them. You will have a chance to check out the workplace to see how **ECO-FRIENDLY** it is. Just be tactful—your parent might not want to lose a job (and income) because you decided to tell their employer just how **unECO-**

EFFECTIVE they are. There is a better way to make your point. When you get home, make a list of your **ECO-ACTION** suggestions and share them with your mom or dad. If they think you have a good point and helpful suggestions that they can share with their fellow employees or employer, help them write a letter or e-mail that they can pass along.

By writing this book and **ECHOing** with you, I hope that we're starting the process. We're all going to need one another to come up with great ideas and possible solutions. I want to hear from you so that I can **ECHO** your ideas in my next book and on my Web Site at www.eco-effect.net. I'll also be creating **ECO-EFFECT** lessons for schools, so be sure to ask your teachers to **ECHO** their ideas to me, as well.

Every year, young people—people like you and your classmates—are asked to participate in science fairs or contests. This year, why not try to come up with **ECO-EFFECT** projects? Who knows—your idea might not only win you a prize, but it might also make the world a better place. That's really taking the **ECO-EFFECT** to a higher level!

As one last exercise, go to the Internet and see if you can discover anything **ECO-FRIENDLY** that has been created or invented by a young person. E-mail your findings to me at www.eco-effect.net.

Our goal is to **ECHO**, and to keep **ECHOing** to one another—making our world a healthier, better place to live. In fact, I'm counting on you to **ECHO**. Please don't let me, yourself, our planet and all its inhabitants down. Do your part and spread the word. That shouldn't be too hard—you are an **ECO-ACTION** Hero, after all.

Sources That Have ECHOed to Us:

Artificial Grass:
Eco Alliance – www.ecowaterlessgrass.com

Cars/Fuel:
Fuel Economy – www.fueleconomy.gov

Alternative Fuels/Biodiesel – www.biodiesel.org

Compact Fluorescent Light Bulbs:
ENERGY STAR –
www.energystar.gov/index.cfm?c=cfls.pr_cfls

Composting:
How to Compost – www.howtocompost.org

Commercial Composting locations –
http://www.findacomposter.com

To Find a Group That Will Compost for You –
www.stopwaste.org

Building a Compost Heap –
http://monsterguide.net/how-to-build-a-compost-bin

Decoding Plastic Bottle Symbols:
Healthy Child Health World –
http://healthychild.org/blog/comments/know_your_plastics

Drying Clothes:
http://energyboomer.typepad.com/energyboomer/clothes_drying/

Eco-Friendly Destinations/Travel Information:
www.GlobeAware.org
www.responsibletravel.com
www.GapAdventures.com
www.ecoTrotters.com

Eco-Friendliness of Gadgets:
EPEAT – www.epeat.net

Energy Audit:
Energy Savers –
www.eere.energy.gov/consumer/your_ home/energy_audits/index.cfm/mytopic=11170

ENERGY STAR Program:
ENERGY STAR –
www.energystar.gov/index.cfm?c=cfls.pr_cfls

Energy Use of U.S. Consumer Electronics at the End of the 20th Century:
Data Study – http://eetd.lbl.gov/EA/Reports/46212

Feeding the Hungry:
D.C. Central Kitchen – www.dccentralkitchen.org

Gardening:
Ladybugs –
http://www.discoverlife.org/ladybug/lost_ ladybugs.html

General Green Ideas:
Smart2begreen –
www.greentips@smart2begreen.com

Greenhouse Gas:
Equivalencies Calculator –
www.epa.gov/cleanenergy/energy-resources/calculator.html

Personal or Family's Greenhouse Gas Emissions Calculator –
www.epa.gov/climatechange/emissions/ind_calculator.html

Kids:
Con Edison Kids – www.coned.com/kids/

Recycling Facts and Trivia –
www.ecy.wa.gov/programs/swfa/kidspage/trivia.html

Ice Floe Game – www.nationalgridfloe.com/

ENERGY STAR Kids –
http://www.energystar.gov/index.cfm?c=kids.kids_index

National Grid's Information-Packed Web Site:
Think Smart Think Green –
www.thinksmartthinkgreen.com

National Resources Defense Council:
Simple Steps –
http://www.simplesteps.org/content/category/1/16/38/

Public Transportation:
Calculate the cost of your daily commute –
http://rideworks.com/rwcalc2.htm

Recycling:
Earth 911 – www.earth911.org

Top 10 Reasons and Things to Recycle – www.nrc-recycle.org/consumers.aspx

U.S. Environmental Protection Agency – www.epa.gov/epawaste/index.htm

Recycling Trivia – www.cityofmesa.org/waste/Trivia.aspx

A Little Recycling Trivia – http://paperwaste.wordpress.com/2008/01/08/a-little-recycling-trivia/

www.panasonic.com/environment

Saving/Conserving Energy:
Energy Savers – www.eere.energy.gov/consumer/tips/about.html

Con Edison – www.coned.com/thepowerofgreen/100tips.asp

Home Insulation – www.energysavers.gov

Recommended Amount of Home Insulation – www.eere.energy.gov/consumer/your_home/insulation_airsealing/index.cfm/mytopic=11350

www.energysavers.gov/financial/70020.html

Green Schools:
Alliance to Save Energy – http://ase.org/greenschools

The Green School Act – http://ecochildsplay.com/2008/07/the-green-schools-act-will-lessen-your-childs-carbon footprint

Simple Steps to Greener Living:
www.smart2begreen.com/

Tax Credits for Improving Your Home's Efficiency:
ENERGY STAR – www.energystar.gov

Government and Utility Companies – www.energytaxincentives.org

The Power of Green Game:
www.coned.com

Thirteen Simple Ways to Lower Your Electric Bill:
SmartMoney Online – www.smartmoney.com/deal-of-the day/index.cfm?story=20080423-save-on-electricity

Water:
American Water Works Association – www.awwa.org

Drink Tap – www.DrinkTap.org

Gardening – www.chelseagreen.com